Study Guide to Accompany

NDERSTANDIN
OMPUTER

mmodore Grace Murray Hopper
d States Navy

Professor Steven L. Mandell
Bowling Green State University

B.85

B.71.

WEST PUBLISHING COMPANY
Saint Paul   New York   Los Angeles   San Francisco

COPYRIGHT © 1984 by WEST PUBLISHING CO.
50 West Kellogg Boulevard
P.O. Box 43526
St. Paul, MN 55164

CONTENTS

                                                                    Page
Preface   v

Chapter 1 An Invitation to Computers   1
Chapter 2 The Machine Itself: Hardware 11
Chapter 3 The Computer: What It Is and How It Works 21
Chapter 4 Communicating with the Computer: Programming 31
Chapter 5 Microcomputer Revolution 41
Chapter 6 Solving Problems Using Computers: System Analysis 51
Chapter 7 Computers in our Daily Lives 61
Chapter 8 Computers in the Classroom 70
Chapter 9 Computers in the Workplace 78
Chapter 10 Computers in Business and Industry 87
Chapter 11 Computers in Science, Medicine, and Research and Design . . 97
Chapter 12 Computers in Society: Art, Entertainment, and Leisure . . . 107
Chapter 13 Computers in Society: Government, Privacy, and Crime . . . 116
Chapter 14 Computers in the Future 127

BASIC Supplement

Section I   Introduction to BASIC B-1
Section II   Getting Started with BASIC B-6
Section III   Input and Output B-19
Section IV   Control Statements B-34
Section V   FOR/NEXT Loops and Functions B-51

PREFACE

This study guide has been designed to accompany Understanding Computers published by West Publishing Company. Throughout its development, emphasis has been placed on providing a vehicle that can assist the student in learning the text material. No design will ever take the place of conscientious student effort; however, the approaches incorporated within this study guide will make the task less difficult.

The structure of the study guide parallels the textbook. Within each chapter the student will encounter distinct segments. A chapter SUMMARY is provided at the beginning of each chapter. A series of multiple choice questions with explanatory answers has been formatted into a STRUCTURED LEARNING environment. Utilizing this technique, the student can "walk through" the material in a progressive fashion. TRUE/FALSE and MATCHING questions permit the student to obtain immediate feedback on comprehension. SHORT ANSWER exercises provide the student with an opportunity to express an understanding of the material. Problem solutions are presented in the ANSWER KEY so that the student can evaluate and diagnose progress.

The supplement to the study guide is designed to support the BASIC programming supplement found in the optional version of the text. The section structure also parallels the text material; however, a slightly different format is used. A SUMMARY is provided and a scaled-down version of STRUCTURED LEARNING is presented initially as a review mechanism. A WORKSHEET is then provided for the student to apply programming concepts and techniques. Two PROGRAMMING PROBLEMS are presented as the ultimate evaluation exercise for each section. Once again the problem solutions are incorporated into an ANSWER KEY.

Good luck!

Steven L. Mandell

CHAPTER 1

AN INVITATION TO COMPUTERS

SUMMARY

Computers in the United States have entered our lives in areas as complex as the space program to areas as simple as recreation and entertainment. Internationally, the computer has also touched many lives. Japan leads the world in robotics and artificial intelligence. France pioneered the videotex system and the "smart card." England, Canada, and China use the computer in a variety of unique applications. Even less developed countries like Pakistan are finding the computer a valuable tool toward modernization.

The modern day computer is less than 40 years old but its conception goes back centuries. Blaise Pascal developed the first mechanical calculator in 1642. J. M. Jacquard introduced the concept of programs with his use of punched cards to alter loom settings and create different weave patterns without further human intervention.

Charles Babbage designed the difference engine and analytical engine in the mid-1800s and is known as the "father of computers." America's first contribution to the development of mechanical calculators occurred with Herman Hollerith's work for the 1890 census and his Hollerith code, a series of punched coded information read by a machine. He founded the company that eventually became IBM.

In 1944 the automatic calculator, the Mark I, was invented. It used electromagnetic relays and mechanical counters and did not rely strictly on mechanical gears. Along with this introduction of electronics to the calculating machines came the use of the binary number system which is the basis of the machine language. The first true electronic calculator was the ENIAC developed by J. Presper Eckert, Jr. and John Mauchly. These two men also contributed to the development of the EDVAC, the first stored-program computer.

The years 1951-1958 marked the first generation of computers; these computers were large, costly to buy, expensive to use, and often unreliable. Vacuum tubes were used for these internal operations and the machine-language programs were stored on the surface of a rotating magnetic drum. The UNIVAC I, a creation of Eckert and Mauchly, was the first computer designed for business use.

The second generation, 1959-1964, resulted with the vacuum tubes being replaced by transistors, which reduced the physical size of the computer and the heat generated. Magnetic cores were used for internal memory. Magnetic tape replaced the cumbersome and time-consuming punched cards. The programming burden was eased with the introduction of the more English-like, high-level languages.

The third generation (1965-1971) found the transistors replaced by integrated circuits on tiny silicon chips. This led to the development of the first minicomputer. These machines have the same capabilities as the large computers but are smaller and have less memory storage space. Third-generation computers were the first to be accessible by remote terminals.

The fourth generation of computers began in 1972 and continues today. Large-scale integrated (LSI) circuits, featuring thousands of transistors on a single chip, led to the development of the microprocessor and eventually the microcomputer. The LSI circuits further progressed to VLSI (Very Large-Scale Integration).

ABOUT THE ISSUE--A question being discussed today is whether computer phobia is sexist. Historical evidence suggests that men and women will be able to adapt to the computer, regarding both careers and applications. Initially, computers were considered an item for men. But both adult men and women must make an effort to learn about this new technology. The early education of boys and girls will relieve fears of computers for the coming generations.

STRUCTURED LEARNING

1.   In its own way, _____ is almost as crucial an issue to all the industrial nations as is military superiority.

    a. agricultural superiority   c. computer superiority
    b. management superiority   d. inflation

    *   *   *   *   *   *   *   *   *   *   *   *

    (c) The computer is used extensively to process the data needed to solve the problems concerning these other areas. As our reliance on the computer increases so does its importance.

2.   Robotics is the science of designing and building robots which can
     then be used in _____.

     a. the Star Wars movie
     b. repetitious assembly line work
     c. precision welding
     d. b and c

     *   *   *   *   *   *   *   *   *   *   *   *

          (d) Robots are essentially hydraulic arms that carry out the
          minute directions of the computer "brain." They are often used
          in repetitive and precise work situations.

3.   France has developed and popularized the videotex system which
     _____.

     a. is similar to a cable movie channel
     b. uses video cassettes to record TV shows and movies
     c. accesses information from a data base to view on your video
         screen
     d. is a movie about a video game-playing Texan

     *   *   *   *   *   *   *   *   *   *   *   *

          (c) The data banks can provide information on the home computer
          screen. In France, it is being used for electronic telephone
          directories, financial services, and a variety of information
          sources.

4.   To speed up the 1890 census, Herman Hollerith _____.

     a. used the analytical engine to generate an estimate based on the
         1880 census figures
     b. employed more census takers
     c. manufactured the first electronic computer
     d. designed a card into which could be punched coded information

     *   *   *   *   *   *   *   *   *   *   *   *

          (d) A machine could read and tabulate information from the
          80-column by 12-row card. This machine reduced the time for
          census tabulation from seven years to two-and-a-half years.

5.   The first true electronic calculator was _____.

      a. ENIAC   c. EDVAC
      b. Mark I   d. UNIVAC I

      *   *   *   *   *   *   *   *   *   *   *   *

          (a) ENIAC was the first true electronic calculator and could
          perform the same muliplication problem in three-thousandths of a
          second that took the Mark I three seconds.

6.   The second-generation computers used which of the following as its
      form of computer memory?

      a. magnetic drums   c. magnetic cores
      b. RAM chips   d. punched cards

      *   *   *   *   *   *   *   *   *   *   *   *

          (c) Magnetic cores are rings of magnetic material strung at each
          intersection of thin vertical and horizontal wires. One half the
          current would run down each wire and only at the intersection of
          specific wires would a core become charged.

7.   High-level programming languages _____.

      a. are more English-like
      b. require a high-level computer
      c. are used in high altitudes
      d. translate one line of code to one line of machine language code

      *   *   *   *   *   *   *   *   *   *   *   *

          (a) The high-level language's close resemblance to English makes
          programming much easier.

8.   The third generation used _____ for the computer's internal
      operation.

      a. vacuum tubes
      b. transistors
      c. integrated circuits on silicon chips
      d. large-scale integrated circuits

      *   *   *   *   *   *   *   *   *   *   *   *

(c) Hundreds of electrical components could be included on one chip less than one-eighth inch square further reducing the computer's size and increasing its capabilities.

9.   The _____ is used to govern the functioning and capabilities of microcomputers.

        a. microprocessor   c. microtransistor
        b. microwave   d. microvacuum tube

    *   *   *   *   *   *   *   *   *   *   *   *

        (a) It is the microprocessor that enables the microcomputer to be affordable and practical for the home market. Microprocessors are also used in microwave ovens, sewing machines, thermostats, and automobiles.

10.   The fourth generation of computer development is marked by _____.

        a. the use of large-scale integration and very large-scale integration
        b. increased memory and speed
        c. further increases in the versatility of input/output devices
        d. all the above

    *   *   *   *   *   *   *   *   *   *   *   *

        (d) Even though no clear cut distinction between the third and fourth generations exists, all these capabilities do distinguish the fourth generation.

TRUE/FALSE

1.   T   F   In 1982, the FBI caught two Japanese firms, Hitachi and Mitsubishi, stealing IBM computers.

2.   T   F   The "smart card" is a small computer the size of a plastic credit card.

3.   T   F   The punched card was the original medium used to input data into a computer.

4.   T   F   The binary number system forms the basis of the computer's machine language using groups of zeros, ones, and twos.

5.   T F   EDVAC was the first stored-program computer.

6.   T F   First-generation computers used vacuum tubes for their internal operations.

7.   T F   Transistors were found in the computers of the second generation.

8.   T F   The third generation was marked by an increase in the physical size and capabilities of computers.

9.   T F   Minicomputers have many of the same capabilities as larger computers but are smaller and possess more memory storage space.

10.   T F   Women are becoming more and more involved with computers and computer-oriented careers.

MATCHING

a. telecommuting   f. Japan
b. transistors   g. magnetic tape
c. hard copy   h. Pascal
d. POS terminal   i. online
e. remote terminals   j. machine language

1.   The computer printout that is portable is called the _____.

2.   _____ has rapidly risen to the forefront of artificial intelligence and robotics.

3.   Sending messages with the computer to other computers using a standard telephone line is called _____.

4.   _____ is the man credited with developing the first mechanical calculator. A programming language has since been named after him.

5.   The only language a computer can directly understand is _____.

6.   The second generation of computers used _____ instead of vacuum tubes.

7.   _____ are input/output devices that are electronically linked to computers but are located at long distances from them.

8.   A _____ is a terminal at the purchase point used to keep track of inventory and sales.

9.   During the second generation, _____ largely replaced cards for input/output operations.

10.   Input/output devices that are electronically linked to main computers are described as being _____.

SHORT ANSWER

1.   How are computers used with the space shuttle?

2.   Describe some ways in which the computer affects the daily lives of people.

3.   What are some of the inventions that led to the development of the computer?

4.   List the characteristics of the first generation of computer
      development.

5.   List the characteristics of the second generation of computer
      development.

6.   List the characteristics of the third generation of computer
      development.

7.   What did J. Presper Eckert, Jr. and John Mauchly contribute to the
      invention of computers?

8.   What was significant about the introduction of the IBM System/360
       computer?

ANSWER KEY

True/False

1. F   2. F   3. T   4. F   5. T   6. T   7. T   8. F
9. F   10. T

Matching

1. c   2. f   3. a   4. h   5. j   6. b   7. e   8. d
9. g   10. i

Short Answer

1.   Each space shuttle carries five computers, four main ones and a
       back-up. These computers have virtually total control of the shuttle
       flight and have reduced the jobs done by hundreds of people during
       the earlier Apollo flights to just four ground controllers.

2.   POS terminals function as a cash register, inventory controller, and
       bookkeeper. Reporters often write news stories on the computer
       terminal; the newspapers then use computers for their actual
       production. They are also used with security systems and can provide
       entertainment.

3.   Pascal's mechanical calculator, Jacquard's programmed loom, Babbage's
       difference engine and analytical engine, Hollerith's census machine,
       Mark I and ENIAC are inventions leading to the computer.

4.   • use of vacuum tubes
       • magnetic drum as the form of computer memory
       • punched card-oriented input/output
       • heat and maintenance problems

5.   ● use of transistors
        ● magnetic core as the form of computer memory
        ● tape-oriented input/output
        ● increased main-storage capacity
        ● great reduction in size and heat generation
        ● increased speed and reliability

6.   ● use of integrated circuits
        ● magnetic core and solid-state main storage
        ● disk-oriented input/output
        ● smaller size, better performance and reliability
        ● introduction of the minicomputer and telecommunications

7.   Eckert and Mauchly developed the first true electronic calculator
        (the ENIAC), the first stored-program computer (the EDVAC), and the
        first commercially produced digital computer (the UNIVAC I).

8.   The IBM System/360 was a series of six different computers with
        different main storage capacities that were all compatible. This
        meant a user could purchase another computer with larger memory and
        still use the software from the previous model.

CHAPTER 2

THE MACHINE ITSELF: HARDWARE

SUMMARY

The central processing unit (CPU) is the "brain" of the computer and is composed of three separate units. The control unit reads the actual program instructions and controls the functioning of the computer. The arithmetic/logic unit (ALU) executes all arithmetic and logic statements necessary to provide the desired output. The primary storage unit stores data and programs in the computer's internal memory. This internal memory, which is also called primary storage, is made of semiconductors that have their memory circuitry on silicon chips.

The semiconductors store the data in bit cells that are either electrically charged ("on") or not charged ("off"). Each cell holds one binary digit (BIT). The CPU assigns a specific address to the program, to all data that is input, and to the final output.

Besides the primary storage (internal memory) and auxiliary storage (external memory) there are several other types of memory: (1) Bubble memory, where bits are stored as magnetized bubbles on a thin film of semiconductor material; (2) ROM, memory instructions that are hard-wired and cannot be changed; (3) PROM, the memory instructions that can be programmed by the end user but once programmed are unalterable; (4) EPROM, once again the memory instructions that can be programmed by the end user but here can be erased and altered.

RAM is the type of memory used in primary storage. Unlike ROM which is permanent, all items stored in RAM are automatically erased whenever the power is turned off.

Registers are used for temporarily storing instructions and data but are not considered part of primary storage. The various types of registers are the accumulator, storage register, instruction register, address register and general-purpose register.

Auxiliary storage accommodates large amounts of data at a lower cost than does primary storage. Magnetic tape and cassette tape provide sequential-access storage in which the computer must begin reading the tape

at one point and continue reading until the desired data is found. Magnetic
disks and magnetic drums are direct-access storage devices because the
specific data required can be accessed directly, without reading any other
data. This provides faster retrieval than sequential-access storage
devices.

Mass storage, using cartridge tape as the storage medium, retains large
files, backup files, and infrequently used files at relatively low cost. A
mass storage system can mechanically retrieve and mount the cartridge tape;
therefore, direct access is possible but the retrieval time is slower than
with primary or auxiliary storage.

Data can be input into the computer with punched cards, on which data
is represented as a set of holes punched into a particular column and row
with a keypunch. Data can also be input with a key-to-tape system where the
data is stored as magnetized spots on the surface of the tape. A final
input option is the key-to-disk, which stores data on either hard disks or
floppy diskettes. This is becoming the most widely accepted method because
it is easier to use and requires less storage area.

The output of information is either soft copy, read on the CRT screen
or hard copy, produced by a printer. Printers are either impact printers
which require the print element to actually press against the paper, or the
newer non-impact printers which print the characters without any physical
contact with the paper. The five impact printers discussed include the
dot-matrix, daisy-wheel, print-wheel, chain, and drum printers. The
nonimpact printers are the electrostatic printer, electrothermal printer,
ink-jet printer, laser printer and xerographic printer.

The output can also be detailed drawings, charts, and graphs produced
by a plotter. If the volume of printed output is large, a storage and
access problem can be eliminated by using computer output microfilm (COM)
which prints the information on microfilm rather than paper.

Specialized input/output methods have been developed to meet the
particular needs of users. Source-data automation allows data to be input
in computer-readable form where and when it occurs. Source-data automation
systems usually input data with either magnetic-ink character readers,
optical readers or remote terminals and then transmit the data to the
computer. Magnetic-ink character recognition (MICR) devices read characters
produced with magnetic ink that are also readable by humans. Optical-mark
recognition (OMR) requires the computer to scan a paper for the specific
locations of each mark rather than the actual shape. A bar-code reader
reads the pattern of lines that form a code, such as the 10 vertical-bar
Universal Product Code on grocery products. Optical-character recognition
(OCR) devices recognize specially shaped letters of the alphabet. A
voice-recognition system understands a human voice but has a very limited
vocabulary.

Point-of-sale (POS) terminals are used in retail businesses.
Touch-tone terminals require a special keyboard for input. A visual display
terminal outputs the processed information instantaneously on the CRT screen
and is well-suited for a nonpermanent record. The graphic display device
depicts graphs, charts, and complex drawings. The intelligent terminal is

similar to a microcomputer and can be programmed by stored instructions.

ABOUT THE ISSUE--Japan's prowess in industrial manufacturing is a prime concern to the United States computer manufacturers. Presently the Japanese must make improvements with their software production before their computer hardware will become better accepted throughout the world market. However, they are already ahead of the United States in printer and hand-held computer sales. To make further inroads into the United States market, Japan is seeking alliances with smaller companies within our country and investing heavily in research and development programs.

STRUCTURED LEARNING

1.   The central processing unit (CPU) is composed of all the following
        but the _____.

        a. control unit   c. arithmetic/logic unit
        b. operating system   d. primary storage unit

        *   *   *   *   *   *   *   *   *   *   *   *

            (b) The control unit, arithmetic/logic unit, and primary storage
            unit all compose the CPU which is the essence of the computer's
            hardware. The operating system is considered software.

2.   Which of the following is true of bubble memory?

        a. magnetized spots on a thin film of semiconductor material
        b. keep their magnetism indefinitely
        c. module can store up to 20,000 characters
        d. wide use and acceptance limited by its high cost and production
            difficulty
        e. all the above

        *   *   *   *   *   *   *   *   *   *   *   *

            (e) The most common use of bubble memory is for providing limited
            storage for input/output devices and it is characterized by all
            the above.

3.   Functions such as arithmetic formulas are hard-wired or programmed
       permanently in _____ and cannot be changed.

       a. EPROM   d. software
       b. ROM   e. b and c
       c. PROM

       *   *   *   *   *   *   *   *   *   *   *   *

           (e) Memory instructions are hard-wired permanently in ROM and can
           be programmed permanently in PROM by either the manufacturer or
           the end user. Neither can be erased or altered.

4.   When a microcomputer is advertised as having 64K of memory, it refers
       to which type of memory?

       a. ROM   c. RAM
       b. PROM   d. auxiliary memory

       *   *   *   *   *   *   *   *   *   *   *   *

           (c) A 64K microcomputer would have 64K of RAM memory. Although
           some microcomputers allow extra memory to be added by plugging in
           additional RAM chips to the circuit board.

5.   The _____ holds information being sent to or taken from the primary
       storage unit.

       a. storage register   c. instruction register
       b. accumulator   d. address register

       *   *   *   *   *   *   *   *   *   *   *   *

           (a) All are registers but it is the storage register that holds
           the information being sent to or taken from primary storage.

6.   With _____ the computer must start at the beginning of the tape and
       read it until it comes to the desired data.

       a. direct-access storage   c. random access
       b. sequential-access storage   d. all the above

       *   *   *   *   *   *   *   *   *   *   *   *

(b) Magnetic tape and cassette tape are commonly referred to as sequential-access storage because the computer must read the tape sequentially to find the desired data.

7.   A _____ stores large files that are infrequently used but still allows direct-access processing.

a. cassette tape   c. floppy disk
b. mass storage device   d. a and c

*   *   *   *   *   *   *   *   *   *   *   *

(b) Mass storage devices store the files where they can be mechanically retrieved by the computer system. Access time is much slower than with primary storage or magnetic disks but the storage cost is considerably less.

8.   A _____ printer is one type of impact printer.

a. dot-matrix   c. ink-jet
b. laser   d. electrothermal

*   *   *   *   *   *   *   *   *   *   *   *

(a) The dot-matrix printer is a popular type of impact printer. The other ones are nonimpact printers.

9.   The _____ printer has the slowest printer speed when measured in the number of lines printed per minute.

a. print-wheel   c. drum
b. chain   d. electrothermal

*   *   *   *   *   *   *   *   *   *   *   *

(a) The print-wheel printer prints up to 150 lines per minute while the rest print several thousand lines per minute.

10.   Source-data automation allows data to be collected in computer
       readable form where and when it occurs by using _____.

       a. a light pen
       b. magnetic-ink character recognition devices
       c. bar code readers
       d. b and c

       *   *   *   *   *   *   *   *   *   *   *   *

       (d) Magnetic-ink characters recognition devices are most
       popularly used in banks to input data from checks and the
       bar-code reader is used in grocery stores to input the Universal
       Product Code.

TRUE/FALSE

1.   T F   The hardware of the computer consists of the operating systems
              and programs.

2.   T F   Internal memory is called auxiliary storage.

3.   T F   A symbolic name or variable is used to keep track of specific
              storage locations.

4.   T F   A nanosecond is one-millionth of a second.

5.   T F   EPROM can be erased and changed easily by typing a new program
              into the computer.

6.   T F   Random-access memory (RAM) is the type of memory used in
              primary storage.

7.   T F   Registers must be assigned specifically when writing programs
              in a high-level language.

8.   T F   Hard copy is the standard term for permanent printed copy.

9.   T F   Computer output microfilm (COM) is not popular because of the
              large storage area needed.

10.   T F   A visual display terminal displays soft copy which is well
              suited for those who need immediate information but not a
              permanent record.

MATCHING

a. bar code reader   f. plotter
b. source-data automation   g. soft copy
c. tracks   h. primary storage
d. central processing unit   i. registers
e. punched cards   j. semiconductors

1. The _____ is the "brain" of the computer.

2. Another name for internal memory is _____.

3. Primary storage is currently made of _____ that have their memory
    circuitry on silicon chips.

4. _____ are temporary holding areas for instructions and data, but
    even though located in the CPU they are not considered part of
    primary storage.

5. The concentric circles found on magnetic disks are called _____.

6. Data from documents such as time cards, bills, invoices, and checks
    can be recorded on _____ and read directly from this source
    document into the computer.

7. _____ is the form of output that appears on the CRT screen.

8. A _____ produces lines, curves, charts, graphs and other drawings
    on the printed output.

9. The ability to collect data in computer-readable form where and when
    it occurs is called _____.

10. Grocery products are labeled with the Universal Product Code which
    the _____ can read.

SHORT ANSWER

1.   List the three components of the CPU and explain the functions of
      each.

2.   Briefly describe how the computer stores each instruction and piece
      of data.

3.   Why has a nanosecond been described as being 11.8 inches long?

4.   Why are magnetic tapes and magnetic disks superior to punched cards
      as an input source?

5.   What are the two general forms in which output may appear?

6.   What is the main difference between a nonimpact printer and an impact
        printer?

ANSWER KEY

True/False

1. F   2. F   3. T   4. F   5. F   6. T   7. F   8. T
9. F   10. T

Matching

1. d   2. h   3. j   4. i   5. c   6. e   7. g   8. f
9. b   10. a

Short Answer

1.   ● The control unit reads the program instructions and directs the
          computer parts to execute the desired instructions.
        ● The arithmetic/logic unit (ALU) executes all arithmetic and logic
          statements to derive the correct solutions.
        ● The primary storage unit is in charge of storing the data and
          programs in the computer's internal memory.

2.   Each instruction and piece of data is assigned a specific location in
      memory; the computer can access the information by using the address
      to retrieve the contents of that location. A programmer often uses
      a variable name to represent the storage location. Although the
      storage address will not change during execution the contents may.

3.   The electricity used in a computer travels at 186,000 miles per
      second. A nanosecond is one-billionth of a second and electricity
      can travel 11.8 inches in that time. A computer can complete
      computations in matter of nanoseconds.

4.   Data stored on magnetic tapes and magnetic disks may be erased and
      replaced with new data; a punch card cannot be repunched. Tapes and
      disks store much more data and in a smaller space than cards. Also,
      the computer can read in the data from tapes or disks faster than
      from punched cards.

5.   ● hard copy--the permanent printed copy
      ● soft copy--output viewed on a CRT screen

6.   The print elements of the impact printers actually strike the paper
      to make their impressions whereas the nonimpact printers do not
      strike the paper. Nonimpact printers use heat, laser, or
      photographic actions to form their letters.

CHAPTER 3
THE COMPUTER: WHAT IT IS
AND HOW IT WORKS

SUMMARY

There are two general types of computers: digital computers which
operate with distinct "on" and "off" electrical pulses and analog computers
which work by measuring continuous physical or electrical conditions.
Computer systems can process data in one of two ways: online, which places
the user in direct communication and allows interaction with the computer
during execution of the program; or batch-processing, which requires all
data to be input before the program begins execution and it does not allow
any interaction.

The actual processing within the computer is done in machine language.
Programmers write their programs in English-like languages, referred to as
high-level languages, and the computer must then translate them into machine
language. The "on" and "off" electrical pulses used with digital computers
are symbolized with 1s and 0s.

One way that data can be represented in machine language code is using
the binary (base 2) number system. This system uses a combination of 1s and
0s to represent the data. Because binary numbers can become quite lengthy,
a simpler coding scheme called 4-bit binary coded decimal is used. Here
each digit is represented with a group of 4 bits. Another approach, EBCDIC,
uses 8 bits to represent each uppercase and lowercase letter and the special
characters. A final method is ASCII or ASCII-8 which employs 7 bits or 8
bits respectively for data representation. Since 8 bits can represent any
character, an 8-bit grouping is referred to as a byte which is the basic
unit of memory. The symbol K represents 1024 bytes.

To help detect character miscoding errors, a parity (check) bit is used
at each storage location. The check digit is used to detect input errors
before the actual processing begins.

Electronic data processing (EDP) refers to completely machine-executed
data processing. Data are the raw, unorganized facts the computer must
process to provide the information that is usable and meaningful to the
user. Information processing is an unvarying three-part sequence:

(1) input--gathering the relevant data, verifying it, and then submitting it to the computer; (2) processing--the computer's task of arranging the data and making the desired manipulations and calculations; (3) output--producing the results in a way that is understandable and meaningful.

The stored-program concept permits the instructions and data to be stored in the computer's primary storage for faster processing.

The computer can execute only four basic patterns of logic. Simple sequence requires the computer to follow the precise order in which the program statements appear. With selection, the computer must choose from several possibilities by determining which one is equal to, less than, or greater than another. The loop requires returning to an earlier step in the program and repeating the sequence with new data. The looping continues until all the data is processed. The final pattern is the branch, where the computer skips over some statements.

Telecommunications combines a communication facility and data processing equipment to allow computers from different locations to communicate. The data transmitted over the communication channels can either be analog (continuous wave form) or digital (the "on" and "off" electrical states). The most popular form of telecommunications uses the telephone system and requires the digital signal from the computer to be altered to an analog signal. This procedure is called modulation and the conversion of the analog signal back to digital is called demodulation. The modem is the device used to accomplish the conversion.

Three modes of data transmission exist. Simplex provides one-way data flow. Half-duplex allows data to flow in both directions but in only one direction at a time. Full-duplex allows a simultaneous two way data flow.

ABOUT THE ISSUE--Four ways in which computer errors can occur are: (1) using incorrect input; (2) an actual error occurring in the program; (3) the computer calculates an incorrect answer because of the limitations of real and integer arithmetic; and (4) when the computer program was unintentionally designed so that it will not give the same response as a human being in the same situation. With such a variety of error possibilities, who is actually responsibile for the error is still not determined.

STRUCTURED LEARNING

1.   Online systems place the user in _____ communication with the computer.

a. standby   c. direct
b. indirect   d. on call

*   *   *   *   *   *   *   *   *   *   *   *

(c) Online systems place the user in direct communication and allow interaction with the computer.

2.   Computer programs can be written in a variety of languages, but the computer does all its required functioning in _____ language.

    a. computer   c. English
    b. BASIC   d. machine

    *   *   *   *   *   *   *   *   *   *   *   *

    (d) Programs are generally written in a high-level language which the computer must translate to machine language prior to any execution. This is the only language with which a computer can internally operate.

3.   The binary number 10011011 is _____ in the decimal system.

    a. 10,011,011   c. 20
    b. 147   d. 155

    *   *   *   *   *   *   *   *   *   *   *   *

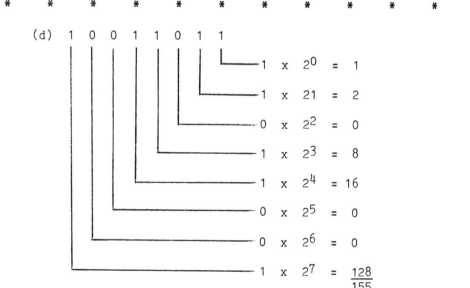

$$
\begin{aligned}
\text{(d)} \quad 1 \quad 0 \quad 0 \quad 1 \quad 1 \quad 0 \quad 1 \quad 1 \\
1 \times 2^0 &= 1 \\
1 \times 2^1 &= 2 \\
0 \times 2^2 &= 0 \\
1 \times 2^3 &= 8 \\
1 \times 2^4 &= 16 \\
0 \times 2^5 &= 0 \\
0 \times 2^6 &= 0 \\
1 \times 2^7 &= \underline{128} \\
&\ 155
\end{aligned}
$$

4.   The _____ is used to detect errors in the internal representation
of data at each memory location.

    a. parity bit   c. error bit
    b. check digit   d. CEC--computer error check

    *   *   *   *   *   *   *   *   *   *   *   *

        (a) The parity bit detects errors in the internal representation
        of data. At each memory location the parity bit is present, and
        the computer constantly monitors its operations to ensure the
        correct number of bits are present.

5.   A kilobyte contains _____ individual bytes, which is commonly
referred to as K bytes.

    a. 124   c. 2^{10}
    b. 1024   d. 10,024

    *   *   *   *   *   *   *   *   *   *   *   *

        (b and c) A kilobyte is exactly 1024 bytes which is 2^{10}.

6.   The term input refers to _____.

    a. the process of gathering the relevant data
    b. translating the data into a form the computer can understand
    c. the actual submitting of data to the computer
    d. all the above

    *   *   *   *   *   *   *   *   *   *   *   *

        (d) Input includes all three processes.

7.   The computer uses the _____ sequence to return to an earlier step
in a program and repeat the same sequence but with new data.

    a. branch   c. selection
    b. loop   d. simple sequence

    *   *   *   *   *   *   *   *   *   *   *   *

        (b) The loop sequence returns to an earlier step of the program
        and repeats the procedures with new data. This takes advantage
        of the computer's ability to rapidly perform repetitive tasks.

8.   _____ transmission involves sending data as distinct "on" and "off" electrical pulses and represents data in the same form the computer does.

    a. bit   c. digital
    b. telecommunications   d. analog

    *   *   *   *   *   *   *   *   *   *   *   *

        (c) Digital computers work with distinct "on" and "off" electrical pulses and therefore digital transmission requires no conversion. This is the most error-free type of transmission.

9.   Which is not one of the three basic transmission modes used to classify communication channels?

    a. simplex   c. half-duplex
    b. multi-duplex   d. full-duplex

    *   *   *   *   *   *   *   *   *   *   *   *

        (b) Multi-duplex is not one of the basic transmission modes. The other three answers are the only modes for classifying communication channels.

10.   Which is a concern of society and business regarding computer errors?

    a. Who actually makes the mistake?
    b. Who assumes responsibility for the mistake?
    c. How computer mistakes can be eliminated?
    d. all the above

    *   *   *   *   *   *   *   *   *   *   *   *

        (d) All three questions are a major issue regarding computer errors.

TRUE/FALSE

1.   T F   Digital computers are those that measure continuous physical or electrical conditions.

2.   T F   With batch processing all of the information must be fed into the computer at once.

3.   T F   Programs written in machine language are not portable between different brands of computers because each brand works with a specific machine language.

4.   T F   Electronic data processing, or EDP, is often shortened to data processing and refers to completely machine-executed data processing.

5.   T F   Data refers to facts that have been organized and are usable and meaningful to the end user.

6.   T F   Processing refers to the steps the computer executes to input the data.

7.   T F   A programmer must be cautious not to use many GOTO statements because they confuse the program's logic.

8.   T F   The combined use of communication facilities and data processing equipment is called telecommunications.

9.   T F   A modem is the telecommunications device that converts the digital pulse and analog wave forms.

10.   T F   The data processing department assumes full responsibility for any type of computer error in its business transactions.

MATCHING

a. byte   f. demodulation
b. bit   g. ASCII
c. output   h. selection
d. stored-program concept   i. digital computers
e. EBCDIC   j. modulation

1.   _____ operate by recording "on" and "off" electrical pulses.

2.   Each digit position in a binary number is called a _____.

3.   _____ is an 8-bit code used to represent uppercase and lowercase letters, numbers, and special characters.

4.   _____ is a 7-bit code used to represent uppercase and lowercase letters, numbers, and special characters.

5.   A _____ is a group of eight adjacent bits.

6.   The computer processes data into information, or results, called
       _____ which is understandable and meaningful to the user.

7.   The logic pattern _____ is one used when the computer makes a
       choice among several possibilities by deciding which one is equal to,
       less than, or greater than the other.

8.   With the _____, instructions are read into and stored in computer's
       primary memory allowing the computer to work at top speed.

9.   _____ is when data is converted from the digital form to the
       analog form.

10.   _____ is when data is converted from the analog form to the digital
       form.

SHORT ANSWER

1.   How does an interactive program work?

2.   When would an online program be beneficial?

3.   Why do programmers not write their computer programs in machine
      language?

4.   Why is a check digit important?

5.   How does data differ from information?

6.   What is the three-step input process necessary to get data into the
      computer?

7.   Name the four program logic patterns.

ANSWER KEY

True/False

1. F   2. T   3. T   4. T   5. F   6. F   7. T   8. T
9. T   10. F

Matching

1. i   2. b   3. e   4. g   5. a   6. c   7. h   8. d
9. j   10. f

Short Answer

1.   An interactive program is stored in the computer's primary memory and prompts the user for input. This interaction occurs once the computer has begun execution of the program and permits almost immediate response from the computer to this input.

2.   Any time immediate response is necessary. Examples are at a hospital to monitor patients or for airline reservation updates.

3.   Computer programs are not written in machine language because: (1) machine language is almost incomprehensible to people, making programs difficult to write, and (2) machine language programs are not portable and therefore cannot run on different brands or models of computers.

4.   A check digit can verify that correct data has been input into the computer.

5.   Data are the raw, unorganized facts. Information is data that has been organized into a useful and meaningful order.

6.   First, data must be collected. Second, it must be verified to ensure it is accurate, complete and relevant. Third, the data must be coded so it can be machine read and input into the computer.

7.   ● simple sequence
        ● selection
        ● loop
        ● branch

CHAPTER 4
COMMUNICATING WITH THE
COMPUTER: PROGRAMMING

SUMMARY

Programming languages appear in three levels: machine language, the electrically charged "on/off" states; assembly language, which uses mnemonics to replace the "on/off" (1 and 0) machine language code; and high-level language, which uses English-like commands.

The set of instructions written by the programmer is called the source program. The computer must translate the source program into the object program before it can execute the program. The assembler program translates assembly language programs and either the interpreter or the compiler translates the high-level language programs into the object programs. During translation any syntax errors caused by violations of the rules for that particular programming language are detected and must be corrected.

Solving problems with a computer is a four-part process: (1) defining the problem, (2) designing a solution, (3) coding the program, and (4) compiling, testing, and debugging the program.

After the specific problem for the computer to solve has been defined, any algorithms needed for the solution must be formulated. The algorithms can be represented in sentence form using pseudocode or in a diagram using a flowchart. The algorithms must then be coded into a computer language program. The program should be easy to read and understand, reliable, workable under all conditions, convenient to modify and update, and portable. The final step, compiling, debugging, and testing, involves the actual computer hardware. The program is submitted into the computer and compiled (translated into machine language). Any syntax or run-time errors are corrected. The program is then tested under all possible conditions for logic errors.

There are two basic types of programs. System programs coordinate the operation of computer hardware, and application programs solve particular problems for the user.

The most widely used system program is the operating system, a collection of programs the computer uses to manage its own operations. The operating system is stored in an area known as the system residence device until it is called into a reserved space in primary storage.

Two types of programs comprise the operating system, control programs and processing programs. Control programs oversee all system operations and perform such tasks as input/output, scheduling, and communicating with the computer operator or programmer. The other type is processing programs, which are supervised by the control programs. Processing programs include the language translators, library programs and utility programs which are used by the programmer to simplify a program's preparation.

Machine-oriented languages seek the most efficient use of the computer. Machine language is the only language the computer can recognize and the only one to which it can respond. The programmer must specify precisely each machine operation. Assembly language is very similar to machine language in that the programmer must specify machine operations. The difference between the two is the programmer uses symbolic names (or mnemonics) with assembly language.

Procedure-oriented languages concentrate on the various processing steps and are designed to facilitate the programmer in directing the computer to perform these tasks.

The most common procedure-oriented languages are COBOL which is used for business applications, FORTRAN which is used for scientific applications, and PL/I which is used for both scientific and business problems.

Problem-oriented languages are designed to solve processing requirements with minimal programming effort. RPG is a problem-oriented language used to generate business reports.

Interactive languages use immediate input from either the programmer or user to direct the processing. Some interactive programs found on small computer systems use an interpreter rather than a compiler to translate source program statements to object code. An interpreter translates one instruction at a time while the compiler will translate the entire source program in one step. BASIC is often used to teach beginners how to program and is the built-in language on most microcomputers. Pascal is an alternative to the BASIC language and is more powerful. APL is popular for business use and has two modes: execution and definition. The execution mode allows the terminal to be used like a desk calculator. In the definition mode, a series of instructions is entered into memory and the entire program is executed on command from the user.

Multiprogramming, virtual storage, and multiprocessing are recent developments to increase the efficiency of the computer. Multiprogramming allows several programs to be stored in primary storage where they may be executed instead of the computer idly waiting while the slower I/O operations occur. Virtual storage permits portions, rather than entire programs, to reside in primary storage thus creating memory space for other programs, further utilizing the multiprogramming attributes. Multiprocessing uses two or more CPUs linked together for coordinated operations.

Structured programming has four objectives: (1) to reduce testing time; (2) to increase programmer productivity; (3) to increase clarity, and (4) to decrease maintenance time and effort. Modules are the basis of structured programming. It should be a proper program, have definitive variable names and organized branch patterns (with limited GO TO commands).

ABOUT THE ISSUE--Programming is considered by some to be an art and by others to be a science, and rational arguments exist for both sides. The final decision perhaps lies in the eyes of the programmer.

STRUCTURED LEARNING

1.   A program can be entered into the computer from which type of medium?

      a. punched cards   c. magnetic disks
      b. magnetic tapes   d. all the above

      *   *   *   *   *   *   *   *   *   *   *   *

            (d) A program can be entered into the computer from punched
            cards, magnetic tapes, or magnetic disks. The magnetic tapes
            and disks are more popular than punched cards because of their
            convenience and speed.

2.   The computer translates the source program into the _____ program
      which it can then execute.

      a. compiler   c. object
      b. assembler   d. language-translator

      *   *   *   *   *   *   *   *   *   *   *   *

            (c) The computer translates the source program into the object
            program which is in machine language and the computer is able to
            execute.

3.   A debugging technique in which the programmer pretends to be the
      computer is _____.

      a. tracing   c. desk-checking
      b. logic analysis   d. dump-reading

      *   *   *   *   *   *   *   *   *   *   *   *

(c) Because the computer is capable of executing only programmer-supplied instructions, the programmers can pretend to be the computer and follow through the instructions in a similar manner. Errors in logic are often detected in this way.

4.   The actual computer program contains _____ which outline(s) the desired sequence and details of instructions necessary to solve a problem.

    a. algorithms   c. flowcharts
    b. psuedocode   d. commands

*   *   *   *   *   *   *   *   *   *   *   *

    (a) An algorithm is an outline of the logic used to solve a problem.

5.   There are two basic types of programs, application programs and the _____ programs.

    a. business   c. software
    b. operating   d. system

*   *   *   *   *   *   *   *   *   *   *   *

    (d) The system program coordinates the operation of the computer hardware while the application program solves particular problems for the computer user.

6.   The programming language used primarily by engineers, scientists, and mathematicians because of its extraordinary mathematical capability is _____.

    a. COBOL   c. BASIC
    b. RPG   d. FORTRAN

*   *   *   *   *   *   *   *   *   *   *   *

    (d) FORTRAN is most applicable in situations where complex arithmetic calculations are required but is limited for programs requiring file maintenance, data editing, or document production.

7.   With _____ several programs are in primary storage at the same time
      and overall execution is faster.

      a. multiprogramming   c. random processing
      b. multiprocessing   d. virtual storage

      *   *   *   *   *   *   *   *   *   *   *   *

            (a) Multiprogramming allows the computer to store several
            programs in primary storage. Instead of being idle while
            input/output operations occur, the computer can execute another
            program. This speeds up the overall execution time.

8.   Which is not one of the four objectives of structured programming?

      a. to reduce testing time
      b. to reduce the number of programmers needed
      c. to increase programmer productivity
      d. to increase clarity by reducing complexity
      e. to decrease maintenance time and effort

      *   *   *   *   *   *   *   *   *   *   *   *

            (b) Structured programming deals with program writing, not
            employment. The four objectives help programs to be easy to
            read, easy to maintain, and easy to modify.

9.   Structured programming uses which of the following techniques to
      obtain its objectives?

      a. variable names that are definitive and relevant
      b. indentation and spacing of the program to enhance readability
      c. all programs written in COBOL
      d. liberal use of comments, statements, and remarks

      *   *   *   *   *   *   *   *   *   *   *   *

            (a, b, d) Are techniques used to meet the structured program
            objectives.

TRUE/FALSE

1.   T F   All programs in machine language are transferable from one
              brand of computer to another brand of computer.

2.   T   F   The source program is the set of instructions written by the programmer.

3.   T   F   A programmer debugs a program by correcting all the mistakes that may be present.

4.   T   F   A flowchart is a brief set of instructions written in sentence form.

5.   T   F   Utility programs perform specialized applications for the utility industry.

6.   T   F   Programmers use English-like abbreviations, called mnemonics, in assembly language.

7.   T   F   PL/I combines the benefits of COBOL and FORTRAN and is well-suited for both scientific and business applications.

8.   T   F   Because of its simplicity and flexibility, BASIC is offered with most microcomputers.

9.   T   F   With virtual storage the complete program resides in primary memory.

10.   T   F   The branch pattern, characterized by the GO TO statement, is heavily used with structured programming.

MATCHING

a.	software	f.	syntax
b.	RPG	g.	source
c.	high-level	h.	application
d.	front-end processor	i.	coding
e.	modules	j.	COBOL

1.   Computer programs are the set of instructions the computer uses to solve specific problems or carry out specific tasks and are commonly referred to as _____.

2.   A(n) _____ language is more similar to English and uses common mathematical terms and symbols.

3.   The original set of instructions written by the programmer is called the _____ program and must be translated by the computer into machine language.

4.   _____ is the activity the programmer does when he or she translates the program design into the particular programming language.

5.   _____ errors are recognized during translation and are usually violations of that particular programming language.

6.   A(n) _____ program is designed to solve a particular problem for the user.

7.   _____ is the most frequently used business programming language because of its file handling capabilities.

8.   The _____ is the programming language that enables a programmer to describe the design of a business report and then the generator program will write the necessary instructions.

9.   The _____ is a smaller CPU in a multiprocessing system configuration.

10.   Basic to the concept of structured programming is the construction of programs in _____, with each one being an independent segment that performs only one function.

SHORT ANSWER

1.   What are the three levels of computer languages?

2.   List the four-part process for solving problems with a computer.

3.   Explain the difference among syntax errors, run-time errors, and
      logic errors.

4.   What is an operating system?

5.   What are the advantages of the COBOL programming language?

6.   How does an interpreter work?

7.   What is multiprocessing?

8.   What are the key points in the argument that programming is a
      science?

9.   What are the key points in the argument that programming is an art?

ANSWER KEY

True/False

1. F   2. T   3. T   4. F   5. F   6. T   7. T   8. T
9. F   10. F

Matching

1. a   2. c   3. g   4. i   5. f   6. h   7. j   8. b
9. d   10. e

Short Answer

1.
- machine language
- assembly language
- high-level language

2.
1. define the problem
2. design a solution
3. code the program
4. compile, test, and debug the program

3.
- Syntax errors violate the grammer rules of a particular computer language.
- Run-time errors occur when one tells the computer to do something that it cannot do such as divide by zero.
- Logic errors are the worst type because the computer will execute the program entirely but it generates an incorrect answer. (The computer can not operate when either a syntax or run-time error occurs and will produce an error message to inform the user.)

4.   The operating system is a collection of programs the computer uses to manage its own operations, such as handling the input and output devices and controlling the program's execution.

5.
- It is machine-independent and standardized, meaning it can be used by any computer that has a COBOL compiler.
- It has very English-like commands that make the program almost self-explanatory.
- It has strong file-handling capabilities.

6.   The interpreter translates the source statements into the object code. It takes one source program instruction, translates it into machine code, and then executes it. It then takes the next instruction, translates it, executes it, and so on.

7.   Multiprocessing involves using two or more CPUs linked together for a coordinated operation. Usually a small CPU handles all input/output interruptions and a large CPU does the "number crunching."

8   Present-day programmers use a logical and systematic approach known as structured programming. This involves the three areas of designing, documenting, and testing programs. There is also a strong movement toward granting software patents.

9.   The early programmers, as well as the novice home computer owner, follow no systematic methods of programming. Also, there is no insight into what makes the programming process productive because their is no quantitative measure of a programmer's work.

CHAPTER 5
MICROCOMPUTER REVOLUTION

SUMMARY

The microcomputer technology developed in the late 1970s and the microcomputer soon became very popular, easy to use, and affordable to the average user.

The microcomputer uses the microprocessor chip instead of the CPU to do its processing. Another difference is that the word size and number of registers of microcomputers are smaller than those in large computers.

Secondary storage media for microcomputers include magnetic tape, cartridges, floppy disks, and hard disks. Magnetic tape is the cheapest medium for data storage but the data can only be read sequentially. Cartridges store data in ROM or RAM chips. Floppy disks come in 8-inch, $5\frac{1}{4}$-inch, and sub-4-inch sizes. They can be formatted single-sided/single-density, single-sided/double-density, double-sided/single-density, and double-sided/double-density. (Double-sided stores data on both sides of the disk; double-density stores data closer together than single-density). Also, floppy disks permit random access. Hard disks can be used only with certain microcomputers, and they function similarly to floppy disks. But they permit more storage and allow faster retrieval. Two new storage alternatives are the optical laser which can store a larger amount of data and the RAM chip which can input data at the same speed as the microprocessor works.

Many input/output devices are used commonly with both micros and larger computers. They include keyboards, printers, plotters, and display terminals. Other input/output devices are unique to the microcomputer. These are joysticks and game paddles, electronic drawing pens, light pens, spatial digitizers, voice-recognition, voice syntesizers and the mouse.

Software for the microcomputer is divided into four areas: business, home-management, education, and games, with many programs overlapping into two or more areas. Business software performs routine tasks such as accounts receivable, accounts payable, budgeting, word processing, payroll, spreadsheets, inventory, and graphs for the business environment.

Home-management software includes a wide variety of applications such as budgeting, energy control, security, inventory for the home, and hobbyist programs. Educational software aids the learning process at all age levels and is divided into three categories: drills, tutorials, and simulations. Game programs are the most popular form of computer software. Computer games can be either arcade-like video games, adventure games, or educational games.

Several programming languages are available for microcomputers. BASIC is the most popular because it is relatively easy to learn and is also interactive. Pascal is also popular but requires much more memory. LOGO and Pilot are new educational languages.

Networks permit several micros to be linked together for sharing messages and information between the users. Networks are popular in the classroom where teachers and students may interact via the computer linkup. Commercial networks convey news and reference data utilizing data banks.

ABOUT THE ISSUE--The Computer Contributions Bill of 1982 was rejected even though the donated computers would have benefited students. It was felt that the computer manufacturers would have benefited excessively.

STRUCTURED LEARNING

1.   The microcomputer's appeal to the home owner or small businessperson is based on all the following reasons except _____.

       a. the price of a microcomputer is now affordable for most people.
       b. They are user friendly.
       c. commercial software is now available eliminating the necessity to write your own programs.
       d. they are a necessary appliance in every household.

       *   *   *   *   *   *   *   *   *   *   *   *

       (d) All are reasons for their popularity except for d. Even though they provide many uses in the home they are currently not an indispensable item.

2.   Data is stored _____ on cassette tape.

       a. sequentially   c. indirectly
       b. randomly   d. none of the above

       *   *   *   *   *   *   *   *   *   *   *   *

       (a) The cassette tape player stores the data sequentially and therefore must also read the data sequentially.

3. Floppy disks, or diskettes, generally come in which of the following two sizes?

    a. $8\frac{1}{2}$ inch   d. 8 inch
    b. 5 inch   e. 11 inch
    c. $5\frac{1}{4}$ inch

    *   *   *   *   *   *   *   *   *   *   *   *

        (c) and (d) Currently the most popular floppy disks are either 8 inch or $5\frac{1}{4}$ inch but a sub-4-inch floppy is also available.

4. What device is used to control the movement of cursors on a TV screen by inputting electrical responses into the computer?

    a. joystick   d. a and b
    b. game paddle   e. all of the above
    c. mouse

    *   *   *   *   *   *   *   *   *   *   *   *

        (e) The joystick and game paddle are used to control object movement with video games. The mouse allows the user to bypass the keyboard by entering instructions directly to the computer to move the cursor.

5. The major advantage of floppy disks and hard disks is that they permit data to be accessed in which way?

    a. sequentially   d. a and b
    b. randomly   e. b and c
    c. virtually

    *   *   *   *   *   *   *   *   *   *   *   *

        (d) Data may be read sequentially just as with cassette tapes but it also can be accessed randomly. Random access allows the computer to very quickly locate and read specific data from anywhere on the floppy disk.

6.   What activates the computer to do specific tasks according to vocal
      sounds fed into it?

      a.   spatial digitizers   c.   voice-recognition systems
      b.   joysticks   d.   voice synthesizers

      *   *   *   *   *   *   *   *   *   *   *   *

          (c) Voice-recognition systems are used for vocal input and allow
          you to instruct the computer by simply talking to it.

7.   Which of the following is not one of the three categories of
      educational software?

      a.   drill   c.   repetitive
      b.   tutorial   d.   simulation

      *   *   *   *   *   *   *   *   *   *   *   *

          (c) The three categories of educational software are drill,
          tutorial, and simulation.

8.   Which computer language is the most popular with microcomputers
      because of its interactive quality and because it is comparatively
      easy to learn?

      a.   COBOL   d.   BASIC
      b.   FORTRAN   e.   all the above
      c.   Pascal

      *   *   *   *   *   *   *   *   *   *   *   *

          (d) BASIC is currently the most popular language used with the
          microcomputer and most manufacturers offer it as the standard
          language with their machine.

9.   Which two of the following are new educational languages well suited
      for graphics?

      a.   LOGO   c.   APL
      b.   Pilot   d.   BASIC

      *   *   *   *   *   *   *   *   *   *   *   *

(a) and (b) LOGO and Pilot are educational languages that can be easily taught to children.

10. When two or more computers are linked together for sharing messages and information a _____ is formed?

a. data base
b. network

c. home management system
d. data bank

* * * * * * * * * * * *

(b) Networks are formed for sharing messages and information between computers. A network used in the classroom allows the students and teachers to interact via the computer systems.

TRUE/FALSE

1. T F The first microcomputer was developed in the late 1970s.

2. T F The microprocessor provides the same capability for the microcomputer as the CPU does for larger computers.

3. T F Microcomputers are generally restricted to a wordsize of 8 or 16 bits.

4. T F Cartridges used for computers can be RAM devices which are erased when the power is shut off.

5. T F The optical laser disk can be erased and new data added.

6. T F The RAM chip is the only storage device that can input data as fast as ROM.

7. T F Software programs often have other applications besides the one for which it was originally intended.

8. T F Drills are educational packages that present short passages of material, then question you on the contents somewhat like electronic flashcards.

9. T F A program written in BASIC is universal and can run on any microcomputer without being revised.

10. T F Apple, Inc. has offered to donate 200 million microcomputers America's schools.

MATCHING

a. adventure   f. Pascal
b. microprocessor   g. keyboard
c. light pen   h. network
d. data banks   i. tutorial
e. buffer   j. video

1. The _____ is the "brain" of the microcomputer similar to the CPU in large computers.

2. The most common input device is the _____.

3. A(n) _____ can be connected between the computer and printer to "hold" the processed data and feed it to the printer, enabling the computer to continue execution.

4. The _____ allows the user to "draw" and alter designs on the display terminal.

5. A program that presents a large amount of material geared toward explaining concepts or steps and then tests the student's retention of that material is called a(n) _____ program.

6. The arcade-like _____ games are characterized by fast action and excellent graphics.

7. _____ games are long playing games that require the players to make careful decisions regarding their possessions, their surroundings and, their companions.

8. _____ vies with BASIC for popularity as a language for microcomputers but requires considerably more memory storage.

9. Microcomputers can be linked together into a(n) _____ for sharing messages and information.

10. _____ are commercial networks for conveying news and reference data.

SHORT ANSWER

1.   What are some major differences between a minicomputer or mainframe
      computer and the microcomputer?

2.   What are the advantages of using cassette tape for auxiliary storage?

3.   List the four disk formats available regarding sides and density.

4.   What are the advantages of floppy disks over cassette tapes?

5.   What are the two major advantages of hard disks over floppy disks?

6.   List some areas in which business software is used.

7.   Home-management software can cover a wide variety of uses. List some
      popular applications.

8.   Why did the Computer Contributions Bill of 1982 not pass?

ANSWER KEY

True/False

1. T   2. F   3. T   4. T   5. F   6. T   7. T   8. T
9. F   10. F

Matching

1. b   2. g   3. e   4. c   5. i   6. j   7. a   8. f
9. h   10. d

Short Answer

1.   The larger computers can hold more complex sets of instructions and
       execute them faster, has a larger word size, can accommodate multiple
       users simultaneously, and has more and larger registers.

2.   ● inexpensive
       ● can be used with a standard cassette tape player
       ● not as intimidating because of user familiarity with cassette tapes

3.   1. single-sided/single-density
       2. single-sided/double-density
       3. double-sided/single-density
       4. double-sided/double-density

4.   ● greater storage capacity
       ● permits random access
       ● reading from or writing to floppy disk is much faster

5.   ● greater storage space
       ● faster retrieval

6.   ● accounting
       ● budgeting
       ● planning and tax calculation
       ● payroll
       ● inventory
       ● word processing
       ● chart and graph generating

7.   ● budgeting
       ● coupon management
       ● energy control
       ● security
       ● various inventory programs
       ● income tax
       ● resume-writers
       ● many hobbyist programs

8.   One major complaint was the contention Apple would use the give-away
       to rid itself of surplus computers and write them off as educational
       donations. The actual amount of the taxbreak was another factor.
       The final reason was a clause raising the current maximum corporate
       donations from 10 percent to 30 percent of the year's profits.

CHAPTER 6
SOLVING PROBLEMS USING COMPUTERS: SYSTEM ANALYSIS

SUMMARY

     A system is a grouping of organizationally related elements working
toward a common goal. Similar to a computer, a system has its own inputs,
processes, outputs, and feedback (which is the response or reaction to what
is occurring within the system). There is a three step process to
developing an information system: (1) system analysis; (2) system design;
and (3) system implementation.
     System analysis is the initial examination of the current information
system. Internal information sources consist of interviews, flowcharts of
the present system, questionnaires, and formal reports. External
information sources include books on system operations, case studies of
other systems, business periodicals, product brochures and specifications,
customers, and suppliers. The focus of the data analysis is on why certain
operations and procedures occur. A system flowchart, grid chart, data
analysis sheet and decision-logic table can help simplify the analyzed
results of the investigation.
     In the system design phase, a new system is designed to meet the goals
outlined in the system analysis and overcome any shortcomings of the previous
system.
     The final phase, system implementation, involves installing the new
system. The implementation can occur in one of four methods: (1) parallel
conversion; (2) pilot conversion; (3) phased conversion; and (4) crash
conversion. A review is finally conducted after the new system is in
operation to detect any strengths or weaknesses.
     A management information system (MIS) is an information gathering and
dispensing network that uses the computer to help managers make decisions.
     There are three levels of management: (1) top-level; (2) middle-level;
and (3) lower-level. Each level has different information needs.
     Top-level management deals with strategic, long-range decisions
concerning the future. Middle-level carries the directives of the top level
and therefore needs its information faster and in greater detail.

Lower-level management uses the computer almost daily to gather information aimed at getting specific jobs done.

Information to help management often comes in the form of a report. Common types of reports are: (1) scheduled; (2) exception; (3) predictive; and (4) demand.

The MIS attempts to provide concise, relevant information to management. Therefore it must organize and store data in either files or data bases. Files result in much duplication of data if each department maintains its own files. A data base allows data to be stored independently according to its own characteristics and the data is not associated with a specific application. Three kinds of designs are involved in organizing data for a data base: (1) physical, (2) logical, and (3) application. The data-base management system is the set of programs that makes accessing the data base easier.

Systems can organize data either with a centralized approach or with distributed computing approach. The centralized approach places all the processing resources in a single place. The distributed computing approach locates the processing resources within the various user departments.

ABOUT THE ISSUE--Transborder data flow is the flow of data across country borders. The problem though is this information cannot be monitored by those countries involved.

STRUCTURED LEARNING

1.   Which of the four elements of system dynamics is concerned with responses and reactions to what is happening within a system?

    a. input   c. process
    b. output   d. feedback

*   *   *   *   *   *   *   *   *   *   *   *

    (d) Feedback refers to the responses and reactions to the system. It may be requested or spontaneous and is a guidance and correction mechanism to keep a system on its stated course.

2.   Which of the following is a source of external data?

    a. customers and suppliers
    b. business periodicals
    c. product brochures and specifications
    d. all the above
    e. b and c

*   *   *   *   *   *   *   *   *   *   *   *

(d) All are sources of external data.

3. Which chart or diagram is used to indicate the relationship among different components of a system?

    a. flowchart
    b. grid chart
    c. data analysis sheet

    d. decision-logic table
    e. all the above

    *   *   *   *   *   *   *   *   *   *   *   *

    (b) The grid chart shows the relationship among the different components of a system and allows the analyst to question this relationship.

4. Which conversion process installs and operates the new system concurrently with the old one until the new system has proven itself?

    a. pilot conversion
    b. phased conversion
    c. parallel conversion

    d. crash conversion
    e. all the above

    *   *   *   *   *   *   *   *   *   *   *   *

    (c) Parallel conversion runs the new system concurrently with the old system until the new one is able to replace the old system.

5. Which of the following is not a characteristic of a management information system?

    a. capacity for expansion and future growth
    b. decision-oriented reports
    c. reports that meet the users needs
    d. producing as much information as possible

    *   *   *   *   *   *   *   *   *   *   *   *

    (d) Information overload is just as bad as too little information.

6.   At what level of management is the computer used to assist in the
       daily operational decisions?

       a. top-level management   c. lower-level management
       b. middle-level management   d. all the above

       *   *   *   *   *   *   *   *   *   *   *   *

       (c) Lower-level management uses the computer for such daily
       activities as inventory, accounts receivable, accounts payable,
       assigning worker tasks, and preparing invoices.

7.   Middle-level management is characterized by which of the following
       responses regarding their use of data processing?

       a. The computer is used on a weekly or monthly time horizon.
       b. The information is more detailed than for top-level.
       c. While top-level tells what must be done middle-level management
           actually uses the computer to decide how.
       d. b and c
       e. all the above

       *   *   *   *   *   *   *   *   *   *   *   *

       (e) All the above characterize middle-level managements use of
       the computer and its information.

8.   Which reports are produced at regular and agreed-upon intervals to
       help monitor the on-going functions of an organization?

       a. scheduled reports   c. predictive reports
       b. exception reports   d. demand reports

       *   *   *   *   *   *   *   *   *   *   *   *

       (a) Scheduled reports are produced at regular and agreed-upon
       times. Managers stay informed on production, use of work time,
       raw materials on hand, inventory, and so on. The data from
       scheduled reports are often the basis for other types of reports.

9.   Application design can best be described by which of the following?

      a.   the physical way that data are stored or retrieved
      b.   the method of how data are viewed by application programs and
           users
      c.   how the data will actually be used by application programs
      d.   none of the above

      *   *   *   *   *   *   *   *   *   *   *   *

      (c) Application design looks at how the data will actually be
      used by the application programs. Not only current programs but
      future applications should be considered.

TRUE/FALSE

1.   T F   The system analysis can occur without any reference to or use
             of a computer system.

2.   T F   The grid chart highlights the relationship between input and
             output documents.

3.   T F   The decision-logic table lists conditions under which certain
             actions can and should be taken.

4.   T F   System implementation is the phase that studies the old
             system to determine if a new system is feasible.

5.   T F   The review process that occurs during the system
             implementation phase can be ignored if the analyst feels
             confident about the new system.

6.   T F   The focus of top-level management is with the future and it
             uses the computer for long-range planning.

7.   T F   Lower-level management uses the computer daily to accomplish
             its specific jobs.

8.   T F   More information is not necessarily useful unless it is
             concise and relevant to managers.

9.   T F   A data base stores information that is dependent and
             associated with a specific application program.

10.   T F   As much information as possible should be kept online because
             it is inexpensive.

MATCHING

a.	phased	f.	MIS
b.	exception	g.	system
c.	system flowchart	h.	distributed
d.	transborder	i.	DBMS
e.	data base	j.	demand

1. A(n) _____ is a grouping of organizationally related elements working toward a common goal.

2. The visual diagram that traces the movement of data within an information system from its origin to its point of use is the _____.

3. _____ conversion gradually replaces the old system with the new one a small piece at a time.

4. A _____ is an information gathering and dispensing network that uses the computer to help managers make better decisions.

5. The _____ report is used in order to supply information on an unexpected situation.

6. A _____ report is issued upon demand by management to answer a specific question.

7. The centralized storage of data that permits all authorized programs and users to draw data from it is called a(n) _____.

8. A(n) _____ is a set of programs that makes the data base contents easily accessible to the users.

9. With the _____ computing approach, the data processing resources are located at the various departments that will be using them.

10. _____ data flow literally means data flow across borders via telecommunication.

SHORT ANSWER

1.   List the four elements involved in system dynamics.

2.   List the three steps involved in developing an information system.

3.   What are some sources for internal information to use during the
      system analysis phase.

4.   List briefly the functions of the analyst during the system design
      stage.

5.   List and describe the four types of management reports.

6.   How do record and field relate to file organization?

7.   What is the difference between physical data design and logical data design?

8.   Describe the centralized approach to a data processing department.

9.   Describe the distributed approach to a data processing department.

ANSWER KEY

True/False

1. T   2. F   3. T   4. F   5. F   6. T   7. T   8. T
9. F   10. F

Matching

1. g   2. c   3. a   4. f   5. b   6. j   7. e   8. i
9. h   10. d

Short Answer

1.   1. input
        2. output
        3. process
        4. feedback

2.   1. system analysis
        2. system design
        3. system implementation

3.   Some sources of internal information are interviews with users of the
        system, flowcharts of the present system, questionnaires, and formal
        reports.

4.   • the analyst reappraises the goals of the new system
        • creates a system model
        • develops alternatives
        • accesses any organizational restrictions
        • estimates what the cost/benefit balance will be
        • prepares the design report and recommendation

5.   1. Scheduled report - produced at regular and agreed-upon intervals.
          Useful for monitoring the ongoing functions of an organization.
       2. Exception report - required by management in order to take action
          on something that is unexpected.
       3. Predictive report - similar to the exception report but is
          directed at a problem out of the ordinary. Usually answers a
          "What if...?" type situation.
       4. Demand report - a report that is issued upon demand to confirm
          or contradict a management suspicion.

6.   A field is each of the individual data items that are stored in the
       file. A record is a collection of these fields that relate to a
       single unit. The file is therefore composed of a collection of
       records.

7.   Physical data design is concerned with how the data is physically
       stored and how it is retrieved from storage. Logical data design
       concerns how the data is viewed by the user or application program.

8.   The centralized approach puts all data processing resources in a
       single physical location or department.

9.   The distributed approach places the data processing resources within
       the various departments that will be using them. A central
       department may still exist but it now supervises the overall data
       processing and hardware resources throughout the other departments.

CHAPTER 7
COMPUTERS IN OUR DAILY LIVES

SUMMARY

    Dedicated personal computer systems are used to control specific
applications such as the environment, security, electrical switching, energy
management, and information storage and retrieval. The most common use of
the computer in our homes is as a game system. But for a little more money
than a dedicated game system will cost, you can purchase a home, or
personal, computer.
    The largest volume of software sold is for computer games. Educational
game software has also became very popular; there are games that are fun,
visually attractive, thought-provoking, and nonviolent.
    The personal computer can be used in the home to organize the budget
and finances. There are four ways to acquire software for use in the home:
(1) you can program your own; (2) you can hire a programmer to write the
programs for you; (3) you can buy the software; or (4) you may find a
source of free software. The technology for in-home banking and shopping
exists but it has not gained the expected popularity because of its high
cost and because of consumer resistance. Also, the personal computer can be
used for hobby activities.
    Computer-assisted instruction (CAI) uses the computer to aid in the
education process. An additional benefit to students while using
educational software is they also become familiar with the computer system
itself. Many new books and magazines are available for the computer user.
CLOAD and Diskazine are magazines available on floppy disks. Furthermore,
membership in computer clubs can help users learn more about computer
systems.
    For a nominal charge, online services offer access to data bases filled
with a variety of information. The popularity of online services is evident
from the rapid growth in the number of data bank companies. There are also
electronic bulletin boards available where you can exchange or post
messages with other computer users.
    New developments for the home computer are the mouse, an input device

used to control the cursor, and diagnostic programs which are used to
determine the location and cause of computer malfunctions. Home robots are
also available but they currently have limited capabilities.

ABOUT THE ISSUE--The personal computer is used in automated phone
systems. It also permits you to shop at home. This in-home shopping is a
rather expensive venture at present, though. And this record of your
shopping transactions and accesses may be kept, posing a problem of privacy
for the user.

STRUCTURED LEARNING

1.   When a computer is linked to sensors in the home it may _____.

      a. minutely control temperatures and make the most efficient use of
          energy
      b. raise shades, activate fans and switches, and turn on security
          lights
      c. dial the police should a break-in occur
      d. a and b
      e. all the above.

      *   *   *   *   *   *   *   *   *   *   *   *

      (e) A house that is designed to incorporate computer assistance
      for its maintenance can do all these functions and more.

2.   Interactive, multiplayer computer games can best be described by
      which of the following?

      a. online software in which multiple players can play one game
          simultaneously
      b. similar to challenging the computer to multiple games
      c. playing several games simultaneously through a network
      d. none of the above
      e. a and c

      *   *   *   *   *   *   *   *   *   *   *   *

      (a) Interactive, multiplayer games allow more than one player to
      play. The computer is online permitting virtually instant
      response allowing the players to battle against one another. The
      computer monitors the game and is not the sole opponent as with
      most computer games.

3.   What are two benefits that in-home, 24-hour banking can offer to its users?

  a. instant access to the account balance
  b. checks may be cashed and the currency received at home
  c. automatic bill payments by transferring money from user's account to the creditor's account
  d. unlimited credit terms

  *   *   *   *   *   *   *   *   *   *   *   *

  (a and c) Instant access to the account balance and bill payment are two benefits of in-home banking. Choices b and d are impossible and impractical.

4.   Which of the following titles are ones that use the innovative concept of a computer magazine on a floppy disk?

  a. Popular Computing
  b. Diskazine
  c. CLOAD
  d. Byte

  *   *   *   *   *   *   *   *   *   *   *   *

  (b and c) Diskazine and CLOAD are two magnetic disk magazines and Popular Computing and Byte are popular paper magazines.

5.   Online data bases that offer home information services provide the user with _____.

  a. video versions of major newspapers
  b. stock market reports
  c. weather reports
  d. movie reviews
  e. all the above

  *   *   *   *   *   *   *   *   *   *   *   *

  (e) Home information services provide all the above, which is just a small sampling of the vast amount of information they offer.

6.   What type of companies buy computerized information, stores it in the
        computer's memory, and then sells the privilege of accessing this
        information to its customers?

        a. data base producers   c. memory consultants
        b. online services   d. network news teams

        *   *   *   *   *   *   *   *   *   *   *   *

            (b) Online services create information data banks and then sell
            the access time via a telecommunications network to its users.

7.   Electronic bulletin boards enable the user a place to _____.

        a. post and exchange messages with other users
        b. mail articles for publication
        c. tack business cards electronically to a bulletin board
        d. read magazines via the CRT screen

        *   *   *   *   *   *   *   *   *   *   *   *

            (a) The user can write and receive messages to or from any other
            user who has access to the bulletin board.

8.   What type of software is used to locate malfunctions in a computer?

        a. doctor software   d. diagnostic software
        b. problem software   e. none of the above
        c. debugging software

        *   *   *   *   *   *   *   *   *   *   *   *

            (d) Diagnostic software can locate problems or breakdowns in the
            memory, microprocessor, disk drive, terminal, or printer of a
            computer system.

9.   Which of the following describes an automated phoning system?

        a. can make up to 3,000 calls an hour
        b. will call back if a particular number is busy on the first try
        c. allows users to read magazines on the CRT screen
        d. all the above

        *   *   *   *   *   *   *   *   *   *   *   *

(a and b) An automated phoning system can do these things, but the personal effect of the conversation is lost.

TRUE/FALSE

1.   T F   The basic attitude of people regarding computers is they love the computer.

2.   T F   A computerized security system can protect against intruders by using TV cameras, sensors, and possibly password-controlled doors.

3.   T F   Most home computers have been purchased to play computer games.

4.   T F   Software for keeping lists and files for personal record keeping is not yet available for home computers.

5.   T F   The computer can be used for hobby activities and the computer itself may become a hobby for some people.

6.   T F   When people use educational software, they often overlook the educational value they gain from becoming computer literate.

7.   T F   Computer clubs are organizations composed of engineers and professional data processing people that meet to develop new computer systems.

8.   T F   The popularity of online services is rapidly declining as home computers become more abundant.

9.   T F   Robots are abundant throughout the homes of hi-tech data processing people.

10. T F   Diagnostic software is used to locate problems or breakdowns with the computer.

MATCHING

a. menu
b. tutorial
c. joystick
d. conference tree
e. computer-assisted instruction

f. dedicated computer
g. games
h. mouse
i. online

1.   A(n) _____ has a specific function determined by its hardware.

2.   Most game systems use the _____ for input to move the various
      missles, cars, aliens, space crafts, etc.

3.   _____ have been the most common software sold for home computers.

4.   The list of choices that appear on the CRT screen from which the user
      may choose is called the _____.

5.   One form of educational software is the _____ which instructs,
      questions, and corrects your responses.

6.   _____ uses the computer to aid in the education of the student.

7.   A(n) _____ service sells computerized access to information via a
      telecommunications network.

8.   A _____ has a trunk with a list of main subjects that the user can
      give a responce to on the branches.

9.   Apple's Lisa microcomputer uses a(n) _____ to input information
      that will move the cursor around the CRT screen.

SHORT ANSWER

1.   List the five automated systems that the computer-controlled house
      may have.

2.   What are some appliances in which the microprocessor can be used?

3.   What are four ways one can acquire software?

4.   Banking and shopping at home via the computer has several
        shortcomings. What are some of them?

5.   What is a computer club?

6.   What are the costs involved in home shopping using a computer and
        telephone service?

7.   What is the potential abuse with a videotex service?

ANSWER KEY

True/False

1. F   2. T   3. T   4. F   5. T   6. T   7. F   8. F
9. F   10. T

Matching

1. f   2. c   3. g   4. a   5. b   6. e   7. i   8. d
9. h

Short Answer

1.   1. environmental control system
        2. security system
        3. electrical switching system
        4. energy management system
        5. information storage and retrieval system

2.   The microprocessor is found in all microcomputers and other
        appliances including the sewing machine, microwave oven, and stereo.

3.   ● Learn to program and write your own.
        ● Hire a programmer, which is quite expensive.
        ● Buy a software package, which includes the program and usually an
          instruction manual.
        ● Find a source of free software.

4.   ● consumer resistance because product quality and appropriateness is
          hard to establish via a computer system
        ● the impersonal treatment compared to personal contact with a teller
          or salesperson
        ● worry that finances and purchases may be revealed to unauthorized
          eyes

5. Computer clubs are organized groups of people interested in learning more about their computers. They hold meetings, feature programs, demonstrations and discussions to increase their awareness of computers.

6.
   - the purchase of hardware, either a videotex terminal, decoder, or home computer and modem
   - a subscription cost to the videotex or online services
   - the charge for connect time
   - possibly a long distance phone charge

7. A record of the transactions made and the data that was accessed electronically may be collected without the customer's knowledge.

CHAPTER 8
COMPUTERS IN THE CLASSROOM

SUMMARY

Schools have rapidly been incorporating computers into their curricula. Computer-assisted instruction (CAI) uses the computer to teach the students. While computer literacy has no exact definition, it encompasses an awareness of programming, the functioning of various hardware components, and the ability to use the computer to solve problems. Also computer ethics should be included in school programs in an effort to instill a sense of responsibility in youth as they become aware of this developing technology.

Many parents and educators are demanding that students become computer literate because of the tremendous impact the computer has upon society. Most school systems are struggling with the high financial requirements needed to initiate this computer education. Parents, governments and computer companies are all trying to help defray this cost. As computer technology continues to improve, computer education must be an ongoing venture from kindergarten to adulthood.

Even with the demand for computer education, teachers still have not universally accepted the computer because they fear computer technology. Some even consider the computer as simply a fad.

Educational software is presently not of high quality. Because the rush demand from educators, software publishers marketed inferior programs. The educational software that is available covers a wide variety of applications and formats. New programs are of higher quality and are capitalizing on the benefits the computer has to offer to education.

BASIC and LOGO are the computer languages that are first taught to students. BASIC is an interactive language and is used extensively. LOGO is a powerful language with more graphic capabilities than BASIC. LOGO permits the user to create his/her own commands, called procedures.

Hardware enhancements, such as the video disk, graphics capabilities, and speech synthesizer will give a fresh approach to computer education.

ABOUT THE ISSUE--Computer literacy is an important topic but some questions exist. Are the video arcades detrimental to children and do children become too passive and impatient because of their using computers? Positive benefits, though, of using computers are the development of logical thinking and the availability of a vast field of knowledge.

STRUCTURED LEARNING

1.   Computer literacy courses are being designed to teach students which two of the following?

        a. the circuits in a microprocessor
        b. a broad understanding of how a computer works
        c. how to run every program available to their model computer
        d. the effect of computers upon society

        *   *   *   *   *   *   *   *   *   *   *   *

        (b and d) Computer literacy courses attempt to help the student understand how a computer works and the effect the computer has upon their lives.

2.   Which of the following is not an unethical practice regarding computer hardware and software?

        a. making unauthorized use of communications network
        b. pirating software
        c. using the computer to do homework
        d. invading business files
        e. all the above are unethical

        *   *   *   *   *   *   *   *   *   *   *   *

        (c) A student may use a computer to help do his or her homework. The other responses are unethical because they can be violating the rights of others.

3.   What is the reason that a poorer school often does not purchase
      computer hardware and software?

      a. Computer hardware and software can be a significant investment.
      b. They believe their students cannot understand computer
          technology.
      c. Computers are not like a movie projector that can be used by many
          students simultaneously.
      d. The school systems are waiting until the price of hardware and
          software decline.
      e. all the above

      *   *   *   *   *   *   *   *   *   *   *   *

          (a and c) Acquiring enough hardware and software to provide
          individual students adequate time at a terminal is a high cost
          that poorer schools simply cannot afford.

4.   What are other sources students may use to gain knowledge about
      computers besides the classroom?

      a. They may talk with salesmen at the computer stores.
      b. Parents can buy a home computer and software.
      c. They may join or form a computer club.
      d. all the above

      *   *   *   *   *   *   *   *   *   *   *   *

          (d) Students can learn more about computers from all these
          sources and many others because of the computer's presence in
          their daily lives.

5.   Which two of the following best describe the future trend of
      computers?

      a. more portable and affordable
      b. larger and more expensive
      c. easier to use with many applications
      d. more complex to operate

      *   *   *   *   *   *   *   *   *   *   *   *

          (a and c) Microcomputers are becoming cheaper and readily
          available for personal use. As the technology expands the
          computer is becoming easier to operate and suitable for a vast
          assortment of applications.

6.   Which two of the following are the reasons that software support in
      the educational field is inadequate?

      a. Educators felt so much pressure to rush into computer education
          that they didn't fully understand the suitability of their
          purchases.
      b. Most software for education is sadly unimaginative because
          software publishers rushed to produce programs for this expanding
          market.
      c. Students must write all the software because there are no
          professionally developed programs
      d. Educators prefer the poorer written programs because they are
          easier to teach.

      *   *   *   *   *   *   *   *   *   *   *   *

          (a and b) The sudden demand for computer awareness has forced
          educators to integrate computer systems into the schools and
          software publishers to create educational programs quickly
          without adequate evaluation.

7.   What is the name of the procedure that LOGO uses to create graphics,
      such as an airplane, that can then be moved across the CRT screen?

      a. TO SQUARE procedure   c. movement procedure
      b. Sprite procedure   d. airplane procedure

      *   *   *   *   *   *   *   *   *   *   *   *

          (b) Sprite procedures permit the programmer to determine the
          shape of a sprite, how many, and their colors. The sprite can
          then be made to move across the screen.

8.   We are in the midst of a social revolution, one that will be as
      important as the Industrial Revolution. What machine is said to be
      the main cause?

      a. the automobile   c. the computer
      b. the space shuttle   d. nuclear warheads

      *   *   *   *   *   *   *   *   *   *   *   *

          (c) The computer has filtered into virtually everybody's daily
          life and will continue to be used in new applications.

9.   Which of the following is not true regarding the communication process when using a computer network?

    a. Discussions take longer before a decision is reached.
    b. Arguments are common and sometimes abusive because of the lack of personal involvement.
    c. The vocal persons have less influence.
    d. The participants have a more equal share of involvement.
    e. One person can easily monopolize the conversation.

    *   *   *   *   *   *   *   *   *   *   *   *

    (e) Users face all the above characteristics when communicating via a CRT screen and terminal except e.

TRUE/FALSE

1.   T   F   Psychologists feel that students are attracted to computers because of their fascination with control over something.

2.   T   F   There is unanimous agreement on the definition and requirements of computer literacy.

3.   T   F   Educators feel that access to computers within the school systems should be based on the academic achievement of the student and the financial condition of the school district.

4.   T   F   Some colleges are requiring students to have their own computers.

5.   T   F   The computer is a real help in teaching retarded children because it doesn't get fatigued, frustrated, or impatient.

6.   T   F   The so-called bad kids from the street gangs in Los Angeles have been negatively affected by the computer because they were forced to learn how to read.

7.   T   F   The videotape permits the user random access to data just like the videodisc.

8.   T   F   Playing video games helps a player learn to make quick judgments on spatial relationships and develop eye-hand coordination.

MATCHING

a. tax breaks   f. computer literacy
b. Bank Street writer   g. HMRABI
c. LOGO   h. BASIC
d. software   i. procedures
e. videodisc   j. sequential thinking

1. Schools are buying computer equipment and _____ in an effort to enhance computer literacy for its students.

2. A broad description of _____ is a knowledge of programming and the functioning of various computer hardware components.

3. A bill was introduced in Congress in 1982 to give _____ to computer companies donating equipment to elementary and high schools.

4. Digital Equipment Corporation has created a program called _____ that puts students in control of ancient Babylon to liven up social studies.

5. _____ is a word processing program for children with three basic steps: write, edit, and transfer.

6. The first language most kids learn is _____, an interactive language offered with most microcomputers.

7. Another popular introductory programming language is _____, whose name is derived from the Greek word for reason.

8. LOGO allows the user to create their own commands called _____.

9. _____ technology gives the students access to visual skills, sound tracks, or computer texts and graphics in a number of combinations.

10. Programming demands _____, or logic as we sometimes call it, from the programmer.

SHORT ANSWER

1.   What are the advantages of computer-assisted instruction for the
      student?

2.   What are some "computer manners" being taught by educators?

3.   Why are parents so insistent that their children learn about
      computers?

4.   Why are computer companies willing to donate computers to schools
      even without the benefit of tax breaks?

5.   What are the reasons that some teachers don't welcome the computer in
        their school system?

ANSWER KEY

True/False

1. T   2. F   3. F   4. T   5. T   6. F   7. F   8. T

Matching

1. d   2. f   3. a   4. g   5. b   6. h   7. c   8. i
9. e   10. j

Short Answer

1.   The advantages of CAI are that each student receives instruction
        adapted to his or her learning pace, immediate feedback, motivation
        from sound and graphics, and a less intimidating relationship.

2.   Computer manners being taught to students are that it is unethical to
        invade business files or data bases, to make unauthorized use of
        communications networks, and to pirate software. Besides being
        unethical, they are also illegal.

3.   Computers have been credited with starting a whole new revolution in
        society. They affect jobs, entertainment, and home life. Parents do
        not want their children left out in the race to the future.

4.   Computer companies feel that the type of equipment on which a student
        originally learns will influence his decision when buying a computer
        for personal use later.

5.   Some teachers fear the technology is too difficult for them to learn,
        let alone teach it to the students. Others feel the computer is
        gimmick-ridden or profit-oriented and should not be brought out of
        the laboratory or business and into the school system.

CHAPTER 9
COMPUTERS IN THE WORKPLACE

SUMMARY

Computers are used in many work places. Farms use them for animal health records, bookkeeping, developing feed programs, and disease and pest control. The fire department can gather information on a building's structure, names of people to contact in case of emergency, building addresses, and the storage location of hazardous materials. The computer is being used in the newsroom for writing and editing, receiving AP and UPI stories, and typesetting. But it is in the office where the area of greatest change and potential for the computer exists.

Office automation can be divided into four categories: (1) word data processing, (2) communications, (3) information retrieval, and (4) support systems. The current barriers to the automated office include the price of automation, incompatability of equipment, and human resistance.

Word processing can improve a secretary's productivity by 25 to 200 percent depending upon the amount of typing done. Besides text manipulations, word processing programs may also have a dictionary option that checks for the correct spelling of words. The OCR scanner can input typewritten pages at over 1,000 words per minute.

Communication in the automated office may appear in several forms. Electronic mail sends messages at high speeds using telecommunication facilities. Voice mail is computer-based but the end product is a recorded message, not a hard copy. Teleconferencing permits two or more locations to use electronic and/or image-producing means to communicate, eliminating the cost and time of traveling. Telecommuting allows the worker to stay at home and use the computer to communicate with the office. All these computer-assisted communication systems have advantages and disadvantages to be considered before being implemented.

Information retrieval is a very important component of the automated office. Data base management and text management systems allow users direct access to company information.

The fourth component of office automation is support systems. Personal support systems use computers to keep track of personal work-related information, for example, one's own travel expenses. Management support systems, also, are administrative oriented but are used within company operations, for example, business appointment calendars.

Local area networks (LANs) link together CPUs and terminals within a well-defined and self-enclosed area. The LANs permit users to share files, equipment, and programs.

Ergonomics is the science of changing the work conditions to suit the worker. As computer use increases, employees complain more frequently of stress and physical problems. Specially designed hardware and furniture are being developed to curb this growing problem.

ABOUT THE ISSUE--The communication process depends upon the flow of timely, accurate, and relevant information. This process can be enhanced by office automation. Even though the communication process has been improved, the effects of office automation on human interaction have caused concern.

STRUCTURED LEARNING

1.   For what applications on the farm are the microcomputer being used?

      a. computer-assisted instruction   c. low-cost feed programs
      b. bookkeeping   d. all the above

      *   *   *   *   *   *   *   *   *   *   *   *

      (b and c) The microcomputer is being used on progressive farms
      to do bookkeeping and to develop low-cost feed programs among
      others. Computer-asisted instruction is used primarily in
      schools.

2.   When two or more locations use electronic and/or image-producing
      means to communicate it is called _____.

      a. teleconferencing   c. electronic mail
      b. commuting   d. telepathy

      *   *   *   *   *   *   *   *   *   *   *   *

      (a) Teleconferencing allows executives to meet and discuss
      without having to travel. This capability can save both travel
      expense and time. The executives can actually appear live on
      screens at the locations.

3.   Which form of computer-based mail sends a recorded message, not a
      hard copy?

      a. electronic mail   c. voice mail
      b. record mail   d. all the above

      *   *   *   *   *   *   *   *   *   *   *   *

          (c) Voice mail converts the spoken message into digital form
          which can be stored in the computer's memory. Recipients can
          fast-scan the messages, keep them, or forward them to a third
          party.

4.   Which of the following is not an area where a telecommuting system
      would be advantageous?

      a. in areas where office rent is high
      b. where mass transit systems or parking facilities are inadequate
      c. where the manager must exert considerable influence over the work
      d. when situations do not requiere a great amount of face-to-face
          meetings

      *   *   *   *   *   *   *   *   *   *   *   *

          (c) All but c are areas where telecommuting would be
          advantageous. The main disadvantage with telecommuting is the
          manager's fear that out-of-sight may mean out-of-control.

5.   Which two of the following are types of information retrieval
      systems?

      a. personal support systems
      b. data-base management systems
      c. automated information retrieval systems
      d. text management systems

      *   *   *   *   *   *   *   *   *   *   *   *

          (b and d) Data-base management and text management systems
          allow the user direct access to the company's information.

6.   What type of support system uses the computer to keep track of
      personal work-related information?

      a.   management   c.   personal
      b.   corporate   d.   model and graph

      *   *   *   *   *   *   *   *   *   *   *   *

           (c) The personal support systems help a professional organize
           his/or her person work-related activities.

7.   A special type of network that operates within a well-defined and
      self-enclosed area is a _____.

      a.   satellite network   c.   local area network
      b.   communication network   d.   none of the above

      *   *   *   *   *   *   *   *   *   *   *   *

           (c) The local area network is used within an area such as a small
           office building. The communication stations are usually linked
           by cable and generally within 1000 feet of one another.

8.   What are the two leading physical complaints of workers using
      computers according to the Verbatim Corporation's study?

      a.   eye strain   c.   back strain
      b.   brain strain   d.   wrist strain

      *   *   *   *   *   *   *   *   *   *   *   *

           (a and c) Eye strain and back strain were the leading
           complaints found in the study.

9.   Office automation has enhanced the communication process within the
      office environment in all but which of the following way?

      a.   permits information overload
      b.   increased information reliability
      c.   faster movement of the information
      d.   improved access to information

      *   *   *   *   *   *   *   *   *   *   *   *

(a) Effective communication depends on timely, accurate, and relevant information which office automation has improved. Too much information can be just as bad as too little.

TRUE/FALSE

1.   T F   The office is probably the area of greatest change and offers the greatest potential for full-scale automation.

2.   T F   The fire department uses the computer to keep detailed information about which buildings to set fire for practice.

3.   T F   Teleconferencing is a business acronym for talking on the telephone.

4.   T F   Word processing can actually decrease a secretary's productivity by 25 to 100 percent.

5.   T F   An option on some word processing programs is a dictionary that corrects misspellings.

6.   T F   Word processing equipment can be connected to phototypesetting equipment to improve turnaround time of material to be printed.

7.   T F   Teleconferencing capabilities have existed for about a decade and are widely accepted in all businesses.

8.   T F   Voice mail records the spoken message into digital form that can be stored in computer memory.

9.   T F   Computerized employee services, such as telecommuting, electronic mail, etc., may inhibit the development of interpersonal relationships in an office.

MATCHING

a. word processing
b. office automation
c. personal support
d. electronic mail
e. management support

f. paperless office
g. ergonomics
h. teleconferencing
i. cottage keyers
j. OCR scanner

1.   Reporters use a(n) _____ program to change a microcomputer into an efficient machine that replaces the typewriter.

2.   Full-scale office automation will turn the common office into a(n) _____ with virtually no paper flow.

3.   The message sent from one computer user to another via terminals is called _____.

4.   Executives can use _____ to meet together and avoid the expense and time associated with traveling.

5.   _____ is a generalized term for the process of integrating computer technology with the traditional office work procedures.

6.   With a(n) _____, typewritten pages can be read directly into the computer.

7.   Blue Cross and Blue Shield of Columbia, South Carolina, use a form of telecommuting called _____, where workers process claims at home on personal computers.

8.   _____ systems allow professionals to use computer technology to organize their private activities.

9.   Executives can use _____ systems to organize their business appointment calendar and business-related diary.

10.   _____ is the science of changing the work conditions to suit the physical comfort of the worker.

SHORT ANSWER

1.   What are some ways in which the microcomputer is being used on the modern farm?

2.   List the barriers that are blocking the popularity of the automated office.

3.   What are the four categories into which office automation can be divided?

4.   What are the features of electronic mail?

5.   What are some concerns managers and employees have about telecommuting?

6.   What is the advantage of a local area network?

7.   List some ways to overcome the physical problems created by computer terminals and the standard office equipment.

ANSWER KEY

True/False

1. T   2. F   3. F   4. F   5. T   6. T   7. F   8. T
9. T

Matching

1. a   2. f   3. d   4. h   5. b   6. j   7. i   8. c
9. e   10. g

Short Answer

1.   Farmers are using microcomputers to devise low-cost feed programs, dairy herd recordkeeping, and to monitor and control disease and pests.

2.   • high cost involved to equip the automated office
      • incompatibility of equipment
      • human resistance to the changes

3.   1. word/data processing
        2. communications
        3. information retrieval
        4. support systems

4.   ● virtually assured express delivery via terminal-to-terminal hookups
        ● access from the business office to Western Union Mailgram service
        ● reductions of telephone, paper, and duplicating costs
        ● the capacity to be sent as certified mail
        ● lower costs for next-day delivery than with conventional private
          carriers

5.   The major disadvantage with telecommuting is that employers are not
        sure employees have the self-discipline to work as well at home as
        they would in the office. Managers fear that out-of-sight may mean
        out-of-control.

6.   Users at different terminals can share files, devices, and programs
        therefore eliminating the needless duplication of equipment, data
        bases, and actions.

7.   ● Use specially designed hardware and furniture.
        ● Adjust or tilt the CRT screen to user preference.
        ● Use detachable keyboards which reduce muscle fatigue.

CHAPTER 10
COMPUTERS IN BUSINESS AND INDUSTRY

SUMMARY

Computers are playing an increasingly vital role in business and industry. The computer is used heavily in business in four general areas: (1) Finance, (2) Management, (3) Sales, and (4) Publishing.

In the field of finance there are many general accounting programs that do the repetitive chores of outputting checks, reports, and forms common to most businesses. Programs are available to handle the specific standard functions of accounting, such as inventory, general ledger, payroll, and accounts receivable. Some more sophisticated programs even incorporate more than one of these functions in the same computer program. The electronic spread sheet is used in financial analysis to provide answers to "what if" type forecasting questions. For example, if a manager wants to calculate the consequences of a product price change, he could use the electronic spreadsheet to quickly determine the resulting change: to revenue, profit, and sales.

Information management software turns the computer into an electronic filing system. This system makes file retrieval faster and more flexible while decreasing the amount of storage space needed for traditional filing systems.

Management commonly uses computer graphics to represent data in pie charts, bar graphs, line graphs, and area graphs. Graphics effectively communicate the data so that trends, comparisons, relationships, and essential points are easily understood.

Businesses use the computer to increase sales, record sales, update the inventory after the sale, and to make projections. Some companies even use the computer to sell their product.

The computer is used in publishing to increase productivity in a variety of ways. The word processing program aids with the original writing process. The computer can also then produce the final pamphlet, report, or book thus eliminating many manual steps.

In addition to the business applications, industry also applies the computer in the actual design and manufacture of products through the use of CAD/CAM systems and robotics. Computer-aided design (CAD) allows the engineer to design, draft, and analyze a new product on the CRT screen. Computer-aid manufacturing (CAM) simulates the manufacturing process to increase efficiency and detect possible problems. CAD/CAM systems are used widely in the aerospace and automotive industries. Other industries are beginning to use CAD/CAM systems because they decrease production costs and increase productivity.

ABOUT THE ISSUE--Robots are referred to as steel-collar workers and are generating controversy about their use in business. They are most effectively used in the manufacturing process for jobs that require repetitive or precision work. The first-generation robots possess mechanical dexterity while the second-generation robots have acquired crude vision and tactile sense as well. The automotive industry is the leading user of robots. Some workers feel that they are losing their jobs because of these robots, but management feels that they have no other alternative if they want to remain competitive in the worldwide industry. Also robots can be used in high-risk jobs and dull repetitive jobs that most workers do not want. In spite of the large initial outlay, robotics can be a very cost-effective investment for many companies because they never call in sick, don't require fringe benefits, never take coffee breaks or get bored, and can work 24 hours a day.

STRUCTURED LEARNING

1.   The most common output of general accounting software is which of the following?

     a. forms   d. all of the above
     b. checks   e. none of the above
     c. reports

     *   *   *   *   *   *   *   *   *   *   *   *

          (d) The computer is well-suited to do the repetitive processing and outputting that forms, checks, and reports require.

2.   Which of the following is a false statement regarding the use of
      computers in business?

      a. Computers can store vast amounts of business data.
      b. General accounting software was the first business application to
          be offered for personal computers.
      c. Currently accounting programs are not available to handle the
          special reports or terminology required for a specific business,
          such as dentistry or retailing.
      d. Some general accounting programs such as inventory control,
          general ledger, or accounts receivable can incorporate more than
          one task.

      *   *   *   *   *   *   *   *   *   *   *   *

      (c) In addition to the general accounting programs, there is
      software available that takes into account any special reports or
      terminology that may be required for some specific business such
      as retailing, dentistry, agriculture.

3.   The electronic spreadsheet is the most common use of the computer in
      financial analysis and provides answers to what type of question?

      a. payroll   c. tax
      b. "what if"   d. accounting

      *   *   *   *   *   *   *   *   *   *   *   *

      (b) The electronic spreadsheet can accurately answer "what if"
      type of questions concerning almost any area in accounting or
      finance.

4.   Information management software for business computers allows them to
      have what type of capability?

      a. word processing   c. electronic filing
      b. game playing   d. electronic spreadsheet

      *   *   *   *   *   *   *   *   *   *   *   *

      (c) Information management software provides the capability of an
      electronic filing system. The computer makes file retrieval
      faster, more flexible, and decreases the amount of storage space
      required.

5.   What type of application is a slide show package?

a. electronic file management program
b. graphics display package
c. electronic spreadsheet program
d. data base management system

*   *   *   *   *   *   *   *   *   *   *   *

(b) The slide show package displays on the computer screen an
entire series of graphs in a timed-interval sequence.

6.   Why do some editors in the publishing business fear the use of
computers?

a. Computers make so many mistakes they increase the editor's work
load.
b. They fear they will lose their jobs because of the computer.
c. The increased cost of purchasing the computer may bankrupt their
company.
d. none of the above

*   *   *   *   *   *   *   *   *   *   *   *

(b) Editors fear they will lose their jobs. It is estimated that
40 to 60 percent of an editor's time is spent on repetitive tasks
that the computer can now handle.

7.   Industry uses the computer to actually design and manufacture
products in what two ways?

a. through the use of CAD/CAM
b. with more report generation
c. by using the computer as an unbiased foreman in the production
process
d. through robotics

*   *   *   *   *   *   *   *   *   *   *   *

(a and d) CAD/CAM is used in the design and manufacturing
processes and can even analyze a product prototype for stress
points. Robotics are used in the manufacturing process, often
to replace human workers.

8.   Robots are very efficient but management must remember which two
      characteristics that a robot lacks?

      a. common sense   c.   intelligence
      b. dependability   d.   mechanical dexterity

      *   *   *   *   *   *   *   *   *   *   *   *

            (a and c) Robots lack common sense and intelligence.
            Management must check upon them periodically because they have no
            ability to correct a situation and will repetitively continue an
            incorrect action.

9.   What two abilities do second-generation robots possess that
      first-generation robots did not?

      a. mechanical dexterity   c.   crude vision
      b. tactile sense   d.   artifical intelligence

      *   *   *   *   *   *   *   *   *   *   *   *

            (b and c) Second generation robots possess more human-like
            capabilities such as crude vision and tactile sense--the ability
            to perceive by touching.

TRUE/FALSE

1.   T F   Every business uses the computer in a similar manner because
              there are no unique applications for a specific business.

2.   T F   General accounting software was the first business software to
              be widely used by personal computer owners.

3.   T F   Some accounting programs are designed to incorporate more
              than one task, such as record sales, maintaining inventory,
              and handling billing.

4.   T F   Managers detest the use of computer graphics because graphs
              confuse the meaning of the data.

5.   T F   Personal computers will never appear on the desk of managers
              because they cannot afford the time to learn how to use them.

6.   T F   Computers are frequently used in the publishing business.

7.   T F   Using CAD/CAM, the engineer can analyze the product design and the manufacturing process.

8.   T F   Users of CAD/CAM systems have found that productivity actually decreases because of the new technology.

9.   T F   One of the first uses of robotics was in high-risk jobs where employee injuries were a frequent problem.

10.   T F   In companies that run several shifts, a specific robot must be purchased for each shift to meet union requirements.

MATCHING

a.   "what if"   f.   slideshow package
b.   computer-aided design   g.   robotics
c.   finance   h.   computer-aided manufacturing
d.   steel-collar   i.   electronic spreadsheet
e.   graphics   j.   automotive

1.   The computer has moved into virtually every area of _____, replacing the tedious hand calculations and recordkeeping previously required.

2.   VisiCalc is a(n) _____, a large grid divided into rows and columns, used as an aid in financial analysis.

3.   The electronic spreadsheet can quickly and accurately answer _____ type questions.

4.   Computer _____ represent data in pie charts, bar graphs, line graphs, and area graphs which make it easier to view the data.

5.   The _____ allows an entire series of graphs to be sequenced in timed intervals for display on the CRT screen.

6.   _____ systems allows the engineer to design, draft and analyze a prospective product using computer graphics.

7.   _____ systems enable the engineer to study the manufacturing process to detect any problems that may be encountered.

8.   The new work force of robots has been named the _____ work force.

9.   _____ is the science that deals with robots, their construction, and their applications.

10.   The _____ industry is the leading user of both the CAD/CAM system and robots.

SHORT ANSWER

1.   Why has the computer had such an impact in business and industry?

2.   List the four general areas in which computers are used in business.

3.   What are the advantages of graphically displayed data?

4.   What can computer graphics do that might otherwise be possible in just the written text?

5.   What are some of the benefits of computer-aided design?

6.   List six general areas that can use CAD systems.

7.   What is each claim that workers, management, and owners have
      regarding the introduction of industrial robots into the work place?

8.   In what types of jobs is it better to use a robot rather than a
      human?

ANSWER KEY

True/False

1. F   2. T   3. T   4. F   5. F   6. T   7. T   8. F
9. T   10. F

Matching

1. c   2. i   3. a   4. e   5. f   6. b   7. h   8. d
9. g   10. j

Short Answer

1. The computer speeds up many of the operations that were previously
   done manually, it reduces mistakes in calculations, and it provides
   efficient, cost-effective analysis. Also if one company uses a
   computer other companies must also consider using a computer to keep
   competitive.

2. • Finance
   • Management
   • Sales
   • Publishing

3. Graphically displayed data is much easier to understand because it
   can illustrate information that may otherwise have been contained in
   many pages of data. Computer graphics are also the most
   cost-effective means of presenting data.

4. Computer graphics can easily clarify and emphasize comparisons,
   relationships and trends, and essential points that may be hidden
   within a written report.

5. CAD allows the designer to work with full-color graphics and to
   easily make changes so he/she can test many versions before the first
   prototype is made. CAD systems can also analyze the designs for
   stress points and poor tolerance between parts, saving money that
   otherwise would be spent building defective prototypes.

6. • mechanical drafting
   • engineering
   • printed circuit board design
   • architecture
   • cartography mapping
   • photogrammetry

7.   ● Workers claim the robots are eliminating jobs.
        ● Management claims the displaced workers are being moved to other
          positions.
        ● Owners claim the robots are an economic necessity when competing
          with foreign industry.

8.   Robots are well-suited to working in high-risk jobs such as areas
        with high levels of dangerous fumes or toxic chemicals. They also
        are more efficient in dull, repetitive jobs and jobs requiring
        precision work.

CHAPTER 11
COMPUTERS IN SCIENCE, MEDICINE, AND RESEARCH AND DESIGN

SUMMARY

Computers are saving us much time and money in the areas of science, medicine, and research and design. In many areas of science, large-scale mathematical computations are easily performed by the computer. Two Landsat satellites photograph the earth's surface, then computers analyze the voluminous amounts of data. Electron microscopy techniques combined with the computer produce enlarged three-dimensional images. In other applications, the computer monitors and controls industrial waste in an effort to reduce pollution.

A second category of scientific computer usage is real-time mathematical computations which provide seemingly instantaneous feedback to the user. Emergency management systems are used as monitors in the chemical and nuclear power industries in an effort to reduce the consequences of a mishap.

A third category of computer applications in science is combining simulation and modeling, called an expert system. The automotive industry uses the computer to design models and simulate the aspects of a car's performance. Oil drillers use an expert system to determine the best locations to drill. PROSPECTOR is a geology expert system used to locate mineral deposits.

The final major category of computer use in science is the control of laboratory instruments and devices saving much valuable time in research efforts. The California Institute of Technology uses the computer to synthesize strands of DNA replacing the very costly and time-consuming manual process with a more economical, error-free computerized one. Scientists use the tilt meter and computer to monitor eruption and activity within Mt. St. Helens.

The computer has also proven very beneficial in the field of medicine. Computer-assisted diagnosis combines the computer with the field of health care. A patient answers questions concerning his family history which are combined with the results from a battery of medical tests. The data are input into the Multiphasic health testing system whereupon the results and recommendations are output. Computerized tomography (CT) scanning combines x-ray techniques with the computer for quick, accurate diagnosis. Even three-dimensional composites can be produced with CT scanning to assist a surgeon prior to an operation. Also, a computerized monitoring system can replace the 24-hour nurse watch for critically ill patients.

Besides direct medical assistance, the computer is used for information storage and retrieval. COMPASS is designed to help the pharmacist prepare and tabulate prescriptions as well as store information concerning the patient. Computers also handle much of the clerical and administrative functions in both hospitals and doctor's offices.

The computer is a tremendous aid in the area of research and design. Artifical joints are precisely designed and manufactured by the computer. Architects can use CAD systems to verify soundness in their designs and pinpoint areas of stress. The automotive and aerospace industries use CAD to design, test, and evaluate their new models. Some technical publications process their text and illustrations with the computer.

ABOUT THE ISSUE--Combining the computer with medicine has raised many questions. Will computer diagnosis increase or decrease the competency of the doctor? Will patient confidentiality be lost? What will be the best use of the computer in patient diagnosis? Will patients adapt to computer-aided diagnosis?

STRUCTURED LEARNING

1.   Which of the following is not an application of the Landsat photographs?

    a. detecting mineral deposits
    b. locating nuclear missiles locations
    c. comparing urban areas
    d. helping choose the best oil drilling locations
    e. locating regions of insect infestation and droughts

    *   *   *   *   *   *   *   *   *   *   *

    (b) The Landsat photographs are not precise enough to locate such a detailed location as a missile site but they are available to over 130 countries where experts study them for the other selections.

2.   Emergency management systems use what type of computer system to monitor and control disasters?

   a.   real-time systems   c.   microcomputer systems
   b.   batch processing systems   d.   disaster/evacuation systems

   *   *   *   *   *   *   *   *   *   *   *   *

      (a) Real-time systems are used because they can collect and process data so quickly they appear to give instantaneous feedback.

3.   Mount St. Helens is being monitored for volcanic activity using a computer. What instrument shows the tilt of the crater floor?

   a.   tilt box   c.   tilt meter
   b.   crater meter   d.   Mt. S.H.T.M.

   *   *   *   *   *   *   *   *   *   *   *   *

      (c) The tilt meter sends data every ten minutes to a large computer that shows the trends in the tilt of the crater.

4.   What is the major advance in health care that combines x-ray techniques and a computer?

   a.   CT scanning   c.   radiology
   b.   MPHT   d.   none of the above

   *   *   *   *   *   *   *   *   *   *   *   *

      (a) CT scanning enables the computer to form three-dimensional composites of the object which is being x-rayed.

5.   What type of information about the patient can a doctor store in the computer?

   a.   medical history   d.   adverse drug reactions
   b.   laboratory tests e.   all the above
   c.   doctor's notes

   *   *   *   *   *   *   *   *   *   *   *   *

(e) The computer can be used to store and retrieve information quickly in all these areas. This quick retrieval provides faster and more effective medical care for the patient.

6.   What is the advantage to an architect of using a computer graphics simulation program in his work?

    a.   It eliminates the need to design new architecture plans because the computer does it.
    b.   It reviews the unconstructed building design and screens it for structural weaknesses.
    c.   The computer controls robots that construct the new building from the plans.
    d.   The architect must only draw the frontal view and the computer draws the sides and back views.

    *   *   *   *   *   *   *   *   *   *   *   *

    (b) The computer can review the plans and determine if any structural weaknesses exist.

7.   Engineers in the automotive industry use CAD systems for what functions?

    a.   to design many of the new cars
    b.   to test drive the newly-built cars
    c.   to control the parts inventory
    d.   to calculate the payroll for the engineering department
    e.   all of the above

    *   *   *   *   *   *   *   *   *   *   *   *

    (a) Once the car is displayed on the screen the computer can change it, test it, draw it, break it, and even tell a machine how to manufacture it.

8.   Computer-aided design in the preliminary design of an airplane has made possible _____.

    a.   the design of an airplane with the same capabilities as a bird
    b.   the design of a combination helicopter, balloon, and airplane
    c.   a three-dimensional representation of the plane on the screen
    d.   all the above

    *   *   *   *   *   *   *   *   *   *   *   *

(c) Before CAD, designers had only one method of evaluating a product three-dimensionally, either with a clay or wooden model. Now CAD systems can produce a three-dimensional design that can be seen and rotated on the CRT screen.

9. What are the two main issues at present related to the use of computers within the health care industry?

    a. The competency of the graduating doctors will decrease because of a dependency on the computer for diagnosis.
    b. The computer will go berserk at the operating table.
    c. The computer will replace many employees in the health care industry.
    d. The confidentiality of the patient may be lost.

* * * * * * * * * * * *

(a and d) These are both main concerns of new computer applications in the health care field. The fear of workers being replaced by a computer is almost a universal concern for workers and not solely one in the health care industry.

TRUE/FALSE

1. T F The computer has been welcomed by scientists and researchers because it can make calculations and projections in seconds that would otherwise take months.

2. T F Landsat satellites are used as spy satellites because they can take computed-aided photographs showing minute details on land.

3. T F Computer modeling is widely used in the automotive industry to create plastic models of the full size cars.

4. T F A geology program called PROSPECTOR actually found a mineral deposit by imitating the same reasoning process of a trained geologist.

5. T F CT scans are used to inject radiation into the skull with the assistance of a computer to help cure deformities.

6. T F Computers are used for the clerical and administrative functions in both hospitals and doctors' offices.

7.   T   F   After a computer has created the 3-D picture of a patient's x-ray, it can then operate on the patient with its hydralic arms.

8.   T   F   CAD systems usually increase productivity by eliminating time-consuming repetitious sketching.

9.   T   F   The diagnostic computer, CADUCEUS, has passed the American Board of Internal Medicine's certifying examination but will not be used for 5 to 10 years.

MATCHING

a. electron microscopy   f. pixels
b. CT scanning   g. emergency management systems
c. Landsat   h. real-time
d. expert system   i. computer-assisted diagnosis
e. multiphasic health testing   j. COMPASS

1.   Two _____ satellites orbit the earth taking photographs that may be examined by experts from 130 countries.

2.   Each satellite photograph is electronically composed of tiny squares called _____ that comprise the visual display.

3.   A computer system has been devised to accompany _____ techniques to provide three-dimensional magnification.

4.   _____ systems can process collected data so fast that it gives what appears to be instantaneous feedback.

5.   A(n) _____ utilizes modeling and simulation to process information used in decision-making similar to the way a specialist in that field would.

6.   Doctors can use _____ to evaluate patient data and compare it against normal or standard values.

7.   _____ requires a patient to answer questions regarding detailed family history and undergo tests, the results of which are analyzed by the computer and sent to the family physician.

8.   _____ is the method that combines x-ray techniques and a computer to make accurate diagnosis.

9.   A pharmacist using the _____ program can record and store additional information on the patient and prescription.

10.   _____ are used to monitor and assist in the case of a chemical or nuclear mishap.

SHORT ANSWER

1.   List some of the benefits the computer offers to scientists, medical personnel, and researchers.

2.   List four broad categories for which the computer is used in the area of science.

3.   Explain how an emergency management system works.

4.   What is an expert system?

5.   Explain how a multiphasic health testing examination works.

6.   What are the advantages of using a CAD system?

7.   What are the issues surrounding the idea of incorporating the computer in health care?

ANSWER KEY

True/False

1. T   2. F   3. F   4. T   5. F   6. T   7. F   8. T
9. T

Matching

1. c   2. f   3. a   4. h   5. d   6. i   7. e   8. b
9. j   10. g

Short Answer

1.
- Computers can do calculations in only seconds that human beings couldn't complete unaided in months.
- Computers gather, compile, and uncover relationships that humans cannot easily detect.
- They can transform raw data into graphic representations.
- Computers can generate models and make projections with no emotional interference.

2.
1. large-scale mathematical computations
2. real-time calculations
3. simulation and modeling
4. control of laboratory instruments and devices

3. An emergency management system contains information regarding the manufacturing facility, the products, and the environment. Sensors continuously update the data. In the case of an emergency, the computer will notify the nearby residents freeing plant personnel for more intensive tasks.

4. An expert system is a computer program that contains in memory similar facts and knowledge of a human expert in that field. The computer can support its judgments by providing the reasoning used in reaching its decision.

5. A patient answers questions concerning family health history. A group of tests is then conducted. The computer then prints out the findings. The test results along with the patient's personal history are input.

6. - overall increased productivity
    - higher quality drawings produced by a plotter
    - common components need to be drawn only once because they can be stored in memory and reproduced
    - ease of moving components into different arrangements during the development phase

7. A major concern is that patient confidentiality may be lost. Another is that the quality of physicians completing medical school might be lowered because they may come to rely too heavily on computer diagnosis rather than their own knowledge.

CHAPTER 12

COMPUTERS IN SOCIETY: ART, ENTERTAINMENT, AND LEISURE

SUMMARY

There are other applications for the computer than just the technical processing and number-crunching so often associated with computers. They are even used in a variety of ways in the art and entertainment fields. In some cases, the computer is used to control the houselights and footlights for Broadway plays, the opera, and ballet. And computers may soon be used to notate a ballet's dance routines enabling more exact recording than filming or videotaping can permit. Computer-generated poetry and electronic novels have emerged as new forms of art because of the increasing acceptance of computers in all applications.

In the field of sports the computer is often used to compile statistics for a wide range of activities. Baseball employs the computer to calculate batting averages, runs batted in, and how well certain hitters and pitchers fare against one another. The National Football League uses the computer to prepare game plans, monitor collegiate players, and log player injuries. Even though the computer cannot be used during a game, it still has made football more strategic. Tennis uses the computer to instantly calculate the percentage of first serves in or missed to give spectators a more detailed analysis of the match. The league schedules for professional baseball, basketball, and soccer are also prepared with the aid of microcomputers. The hour, day, location, and any special circumstances for that game must be considered when preparing these schedules. Cyclists even have small lightweight computers available with sensors to compute the speed and distance traveled.

Hollywood has found many applications for computers in movie production. Screen writers often use the word processing capabilities to write and edit their scripts. Also the special sound and camera effects are being enhanced by computer systems. Complete sound effects libraries are stored in the computer's memory and edited in after the filming is completed. Illusions of size and detail can be created using scale models or the multiplane technique. Animation is another feature produced with

computer graphics and simulation software. Sights that no camera or eye
have ever seen before can be created on film because no physical limitations
are placed on the images by the computer.

Disney World uses the computer to control and pace its double roller
coaster for safety reasons. Disney computers also operate a
specially-designed and patented system called "Audio Animatronics" that
approximates human body motion and coordinates it with voices, music, and
sound effects.

Computer music composers can program a computer to play music without
being able to read music. The computer can even assist in album production
by merging the best portions of the different takes. Special
computer-generated sound effects can also be added to the recording. The
computer can save money and time by being a substitute for musicians at the
recording studio.

The computer artist can replace his/her paint brush and canvas with a
microcomputer. One of the most well-known computer artists is Saul
Bernstein, who has won an Emmy Award for his work in microcomputerized
animation.

ABOUT THE ISSUE--Artists in various fields are using the computer to
enhance their creativity. Artists, musicians, and writers commonly adapt a
computer to their work.

STRUCTURED LEARNING

1.   Word processors are used in the arts to do which of the following?

      a. notate dance movements
      b. control the lighting on the stage
      c. create music
      d. write novels

      *   *   *   *   *   *   *   *   *   *   *   *

      (a and d) Word processors are used during the writing stage, as
      well as to make editing changes to a novel. Dance steps can be
      both graphically displayed and explained in a written-type of
      shorthand using word processors.

2.   What is the major benefit of computer graphic systems to the art of
       dance?

       a. It helps dancers with their stretching exercises.
       b. It evaluates one dancer against another.
       c. The dance notation process is accelerated tremendously.
       d. The dancers on the CRT screen will replace live dancers.

       *   *   *   *   *   *   *   *   *   *   *   *

       (c) The dance can be notated as fast as one can type because the
       character can be studied and moved upon the screen as the text is
       written.

3.   What are the two elements a computer requires in order to write a
       poem?

       a. the poem-writing program
       b. a poet
       c. the accompaning vocabulary data
       d. a list of rhyming words

       *   *   *   *   *   *   *   *   *   *   *   *

       (a and c) The proper program and vocabulary are all the
       computer needs to write poetry.

4.   Besides calculating the statistics about pitchers and hitters, what
       other function can the computer do for the sport of baseball?

       a. send signals to the ball players
       b. coach the team better than a human manager
       c. show the path of all fly balls using computer-generated graphics
       d. none of the above

       *   *   *   *   *   *   *   *   *   *   *   *

       (c) The Chicago White Sox monitor the path of all fly balls from
       the previous season with computer graphics to analyze a hitter's
       style.

5.   Which of the following are ways the National Football League is using
       the computer?

       a. to prepare game plans
       b. log player injuries
       c. to monitor collegiate players
       d. to keep statistics of every player
       e. all the above

       *   *   *   *   *   *   *   *   *   *   *   *

       (e) The NFL uses the computer in all the above ways and others.

6.   Which of the following is not an area of movie production in which
       the computer is involved?

       a. scriptwriting   c. acting
       b. sound effects   d. animation

       *   *   *   *   *   *   *   *   *   *   *   *

       (c) The computer is involved in all the above areas but acting.
       An actor or actress may never have to worry about the computer
       replacing their jobs.

7.   The computer is used by script writers for what purpose?

       a. to makes changes and retyping easier with its word processing
           capabilities
       b. to generate ideas
       c. to automatically generate script content
       d. to cast actors in appropriate parts

       *   *   *   *   *   *   *   *   *   *   *   *

       (a) The computer is used in script writing because often the
       script can go through seven or more drafts and each one must be
       retyped. A word processing program then becomes a time saver.

8.   What is the name of Disney World's computerized system that
      approximates the motions of the human body and coordinates this with
      voices, music, and sound effects?

      a.   TRON   d.   "Computerized Dwarf Systems"
      b.   "The Goofy System"   e.   there is no such system
      c.   "Audio-Animatronics"

      *   *   *   *   *   *   *   *   *   *   *   *

           (c) The specially-designed and patented system, called
           "Audio-Animatronics", can imitate human motion and coordinate
           this with voices, music, and sound effects. While its original
           purpose was for Disney World, it stands ready for use in other
           applications when an idea or need beckons this technology.

9.   What are two uses of the computer when recording music for an album?

      a.   to edit the recording
      b.   to analyze instrument tone
      c.   to add special sounds otherwise difficult to add
      d.   to determine listener appreciation

      *   *   *   *   *   *   *   *   *   *   *   *

           (a and c) The computer can be used to edit the recording and to
           also add special sounds and sound effects to the recording.

10.   Of the following, who is one of the leading figures in computerized
      art?

      a.   Nolan Bushnell   c.   Saul Bernstein
      b.   Prince Philip   d.   Lester Kilpatrick

      *   *   *   *   *   *   *   *   *   *   *   *

           (c) Saul Bernstein won an Emmy Award and gained nationwide
           recognition for his microcomputerized animation and computer
           portraits.

TRUE/FALSE

1.   T F   Computers are sometimes used for the lighting systems in the
              opera, theater, and ballet.

2.   T F   A computer is often used during an NFL game to make the best play selection.

3.   T F   The computer can provide both viewers and spectators a more detailed analysis of a tennis match.

4.   T F   The National Basketball Association has always used the computer to schedule its games because this task is beyond the ability of a human.

5.   T F   The new bicycle computers have not yet gained popularity because of their weight and bulk.

6.   T F   One danger with word processing is that it has a tendency to promote rewriting that may not be necessary.

7.   T F   The movie Star Trek used a computerized camera system for its special effects.

8.   T F   At Walt Disney World the computer is used to control the pace and spacing of the double roller coaster to create more danger than could humanly be possible.

9.   T F   In order to compose music with the computer, it is essential to know how to read music.

MATCHING

a. flight simulator   f. ACES
b. Light Palette   g. statistics
c. multiplane   h. sound editing
d. electronic novelist   i. computer graphic notation
                                    system
e. light pen   j. TRON

1.   The _____ is a computer lighting program that controls houselights and footlights in a theater.

2.   In the experimental stage is a _____ which will record dances by analyzing movements and then translating the data into a moving figure on the CRT screen.

3.   An author who uses the computer when writing his or her novel is called a(n) _____.

4.   The field of sports generally uses the computer to compile _____ about the games and players.

5.   _____ is the name of a computer system that controls special camera effects for the movie industry.

6.   COMPSY uses the _____ technique where illustrated sheets of glass gives an illusion of depth to the background images.

7.   The _____ can be used to generate animation for commercials that are filmed directly from a 21-inch CRT screen.

8.   _____ is the addition of sound effects after the filming has been completed.

9.   The movie, _____, released by Walt Disney Studios, used computers to offer sights that no camera or eye had ever witnessed before.

10. The micrcomputer artist uses a _____ instead of paint brush to produce his or her picture.

SHORT ANSWER

1.   What is the reason that ballet cannot be filmed properly to give an accurate description of the elaborate dance patterns?

2.   List the three parts of the poetry generator that a computer uses to write poetry.

3.   How is the computer used in baseball?

4.   What factors must the computer consider when preparing the game
      schedules for professional baseball, basketball, and soccer games?

5.   What is the significant benefit computer simulation offers for the
      movie industry?

ANSWER KEY

True/False

1. T   2. F   3. T   4. F   5. F   6. T   7. T   8. F
9. F

Matching

1. b   2. i   3. d   4. g   5. f   6. c   7. a   8. h
9. j   10. e

Short Answer

1. Filming has not proven satisfactory because it is shot from an angle
    and only parts of the dance are captured. Also the stage lighting is
    often too dark to catch the visible images and nuances which are
    essential to creating the mood.

2. 1. the vocabulary with each word entered according to its part of
        speech
    2. a random-number generator to select the words
    3. a format to determine the sequence of nouns, verbs, and
        adjectives

3. The computer is used in baseball to keep statistics about the
    pitchers and hitters. These statistics are then used to determine
    which players do best against an opponent.

4. When preparing the game schedules for the various sports the computer
    must consider the appropriate day, hour, and playing arena. Also
    specifics such as holidays, and other sporting or entertainment
    events must be contemplated to avoid conflicting schedules at the
    arenas.

5. When using computer simulation there are no physical limitations
    placed on an object. For instance, one object can pass directly
    through another on the computer screen.

CHAPTER 13
COMPUTERS IN SOCIETY: GOVERNMENT, PRIVACY, AND CRIME

SUMMARY

The federal government is the single largest user of computers in the United States. The military uses computers in their training program. The NAVTAG (Navy Technical Action Game) training device helps the trainees develop battle strategies using real information. Another war-simulation project, Janus, trains high-ranking officers in the battle field strategies associated with nuclear weapons.

In addition to the training programs used by the military, other federal government agencies use the computer. The National Bureau of Standards uses computer modeling to prevent fires by studying how fast a fire spreads, how material burns, and the characteristics of the building structure. The U.S. Bureau of Land Management has established a lightning strike monitoring system to prevent forest fires in California. The National Weather Service uses computers for its complex calculations needed to forecast the weather. Hundreds of data-collection programs (DCPs) are located throughout the world to input variables such as air pressure, velocity, humidity, and temperature into the mathematical equations which the computer then processes.

The federal government, also, maintains large data bases of information. The Library of Congress has computerized its voluminous card file system. The FBI uses data bases to keep information on about 50,000 habitual criminals and to coordinate the many leads in complex cases. Computers are also used to track the movements and associations of foreign spies and international terrorists. Another user of large data bases is the IRS which keeps records on every taxpayer and even distributes some of this information.

The nation's air traffic control system will be automated over the next decade eliminating the need for one third of the present controllers and technicians. Medicaid has computerized some of its payment processing, saving money by reducing erroneous, fraudulent, and duplicate health claims.

With the increasing popularity of collecting and electronically storing personal information, the issue of privacy is a growing concern. The major concern regarding privacy is that of too much personal information being collected and stored. Another concern involves the accuracy, completeness and relevance of the information as well as the security vulnerability of that information. The Privacy Act of 1974 is the only major legislation regarding information privacy and it only applies to federal agencies.

The computer plays a role on both sides of crime. The computer can help prevent crimes such as arson and attacks on public officials. The police can also use the computer to organize information on its criminal cases. The court system utilizes the computer's capabilities to access information on past state and federal court decisions using research services such as WESTLAW. But even with the positive benefits the computer offers to the legal system, it is sometimes used by criminals. The computer is used in money and data theft, crimes that are hard to detect and are often not reported because of the resulting adverse publicity for the victimized company.

There are many ways an institution can establish a computer security system but a determined individual can "crack" almost any system. The final area of crime and security is computer piracy--the illegal copying of software. The court system still has not determined the boundaries or consequences of this particular crime.

ABOUT THE ISSUE--A common thread links the personal information stored in computer data bases together--the individual's social-security number. The federal government has initiated Project Match which uses the social security number to catch illegal welfare recipients. In private business the personnel file is a growing threat to an individual's privacy.

STRUCTURED LEARNING

1.   NAVTAG is a tactical simulation program used by the U.S. Navy to teach _____ to the players.

      a. military battle tactics
      b. boot camp rules
      c. navy history
      d. real information on ship names and weapon capabilities

      *   *   *   *   *   *   *   *   *   *   *   *

      (a and d) NAVTAG is a training device that helps teach military tactics. It also uses actual information in its simulation programs.

2.   Which of the following is input into huge computers and then used to
      forecast the weather?

      a. air pressure   d. snow depth
      b. wind velocity   e. all the above
      c. ground wetness

      *   *   *   *   *   *   *   *   *   *   *   *

           (a) and (b) These variables as well as many others are used in
           complex mathematical equations processed with computers. Ground
           wetness and snow depth are not used to predict future weather
           conditions.

3.   What is the main use of the computer at the Library of Congress?

      a. to record overdue fines
      b. for reshelving books
      c. to replace the file cabinets that store vast numbers of library
          cards
      d. to remind workers when to update material

      *   *   *   *   *   *   *   *   *   *   *   *

           (c) The computer stores the library cards as digital images on
           optical disks. Each disk can hold 200,000 library cards.

4.   Which of the following is the FBI's information system that is
      concerned with habitual criminals and their associations?

      a. Investigative Support Information System (ISIS)
      b. Foreign Counter Intelligence System (FCIS)
      c. Organized Crime Information System (OCIS)
      d. none of the above

      *   *   *   *   *   *   *   *   *   *   *   *

           (c) The OCIS is the data base dealing with habitual criminals and
           their associations.

5. In the early 1970s, regulations and laws regarding the protection of
    privacy were enacted to control all the following except _____.

    a. the collection of personal data
    b. the use of personal data
    c. the dissemination of personal data
    d. the transmission of personal data
    e. the actual amount of personal data

    *   *   *   *   *   *   *   *   *   *   *   *

        (e) With the issue of privacy becoming such a growing concern
        regulations and laws were enacted to control the collection, use,
        dissemination, and transmission of personal data. Nothing was
        mentioned about the actual amount of data collected.

6. How has the computer strengthened the court system?

    a. The jury has been replaced by sophisticated computers which have
        no prejudice beliefs.
    b. The computer allows easier access to laws and decisions already
        on the books.
    c. The trial lawyers can find incriminating, mundane information
        concerning their opponents.
    d. all the above

    *   *   *   *   *   *   *   *   *   *   *   *

        (b) The computer can retrieve informtion about past decisions and
        laws that help create a consistency within the court system.

7. Which of the following are ways that a computer is used to prevent
    crimes?

    a. New York City uses a computer to pinpoint arson targets.
    b. The Secret Service uses a computer to store information on people
        considered a danger or threat to public figures.
    c. Computerized bank guards can detect would-be robbers.
    d. a and b
    e. b and c

    *   *   *   *   *   *   *   *   *   *   *   *

        (d) Answers a and b currently are used in crime prevention while
        c is still a dream.

8.   To overcome the time-consuming process of searching through past
      court decisions for precedents relevant to the case, a research
      service was formed called _____.

      a. EASTLAW   d. WESTBANK
      b. WESTLAW   e. all of the above
      c. LAWSEARCH

      *   *   *   *   *   *   *   *   *   *   *   *

      (b) WESTLAW has created data bases with the full text and
      headnotes of the opinions for recent U.S. Supreme Court, U.S.
      Court of Appeals, U.S. District Courts, and state court cases.
      This data may be accessed through many different key words and
      associations.

9.   What are the two reasons that many computer crimes are never
      reported?

      a. They are of such inconsequential nature they are often ignored.
      b. Many are never discovered.
      c. The institutions that suffer the loss do not want the embarassing
          publicity.
      d. The computer can solve the crime without human intervention.

      *   *   *   *   *   *   *   *   *   *   *   *

      (b and c) Many crimes, such as money and data theft, are never
      reported because they often are not discovered or the adverse
      publicity is not desired by the institution.

10.   Which of the following are reasons that may explain the increase of
      computer crimes?

      a. lax security in data processing areas
      b. the increased use of microcomputers and telecommunication
      c. the ease with which sensitive data is stored and retrieved
      d. none of the above
      e. all the above

      *   *   *   *   *   *   *   *   *   *   *   *

      (e) All the above reasons may explain the increase in computer
      crimes.

TRUE/FALSE

1.   T F   Janus, the nuclear war simulation program, will teach officers to "go nuke" faster in order to win a battle in case of war.

2.   T F   Computer modeling techniques are being tested by the National Bureau of Standards to gather information that will help with fire prevention.

3.   T F   There is concern about privacy with the Internal Revenue Service using its mailing lists to help enforce military draft registration.

4.   T F   Computer data banks have endowed the government with enormous reach and power to gather information on people.

5.   T F   The automated air traffic control system being initiated will cause an increase in the number of controllers and technicians needed.

6.   T F   Pennsylvania's Department of Welfare has gone back to manually paying Medicaid recipients because of an increase in erroneous, fradulent, and duplicate claims paid by the computer.

7.   T F   The use of computers for storing private personal data does reduce cost and add to efficiency despite the negative aspects regarding the issue of privacy.

8.   T F   Since the data may be disclosed without a person's knowledge or consent, most people will not even realize their privacy has been breached.

9.   T F   President Francois Mitterand of France has started an anti-terrorist data base to systematically eliminate terrorist activities.

10. T F   No computer system can be made more secure than the honesty of the persons authorized to operate it.

MATCHING

a.	Janus	f.	Inslaw
b.	data base	g.	federal government
c.	privacy	h.	DCPs
d.	social security number	i.	crime
e.	WESTLAW	j.	Privacy Act of 1974
		k.	computer piracy

1. A major concern with computerized national data bases is _____ because personal information can be accessed.

2. The _____ is the single largest user of computers in the United States.

3. The _____ program, named after the two-faced Roman god, is a computer simulation of a nuclear war.

4. To help forecast the weather the National Weather Service collects data worldwide with _____ placed in a variety of locations.

5. By using a person's _____ as a key it is possible to integrate information about an individual from different files.

6. The _____ has been the only major legislation to protect the citizens from an invasion of personal privacy by the federal government.

7. People with a good understanding of computers can easily commit a computer _____ because it is difficult to establish and employ computer security.

8. The Atlanta police used computers to help solve the string of child-killings by creating a massive _____ of the investigative data and tips.

9. _____ is a research service used by judges and lawyers to gather information on past court decisions.

10. A Washington, D.C., software company, _____, has created computer programs to streamline the administrative duties of the court system.

11. _____ is the illegal copying of a purchased software package.

SHORT ANSWER

1.   What are the two major categories in which computers are used by the
      federal government?

2.   How is the U.S. Bureau of Land Management using the computer in
      California to prevent forest fires from lightning strikes?

3.   What are some of the media upon which the National Weather Service
      places its data-collection programs (DCPs)?

4.   What are the three largest government data bases?

5.   Summarize the major concerns regarding personal privacy and
        computers.

6.   List the major issues with which the Privacy Act of 1974 dealt.

7.   What are some ways the computer is commonly used in the court system?

8.   What measures can be taken by companies and government to prevent
        computer crime?

9.   List the three main concerns regarding privacy abuse of personnel
      information.

ANSWER KEY

True/False

1. F   2. T   3. T   4. T   5. F   6. F   7. T   8. T
9. T   10. T

Matching

1. c   2. g   3. a   4. h   5. d   6. j   7. i   8. b
9. e   10. f   11. k

Short Answer

1.   1. simulation and modeling
      2. data bases

2.   The Bureau of Land Management has developed a lightning alert
      facility that uses sensors located throughout the state to scan for
      the positive electrical charges that occur when lightning strikes the
      ground. The computer takes this information and pinpoints the
      location on a map for the exploratory flyovers which will determine
      if a fire has ignited.

3.   o buoys
      o ships
      o helium-filled balloons
      o airplanes
      o weather stations
      o satellites

4.   1. Library of Congress
      2. FBI
      3. IRS

5.   ● Too much personal information is being collected and stored.
      ● The accuracy, completeness, and currency of the information may be low.
      ● Much of the data may be irrelevant for the purposes for which it will be used.
      ● Decisions are made by organizations on the basis of these computerized records.
      ● The security of the stored data is a problem.

6.   ● It must be possible for an individual to determine what information is being recorded and how it will be used.
      ● There must be a way to correct wrong information.
      ● Information collected for one purpose should not be used for another.
      ● Organizations creating, manipulating, using and disseminating personal information must ensure reliability and take precautions to prevent its misuse.

7.   The court system uses the computer for many word processing functions. The data base system capabilities permit an organized method of file keeping. Research services, such as WESTLAW, also aid judges and lawyers.

8.   An institution may employ a well-trained security force and employee screening and selection procedures should be examined carefully. Also, any violation of company rules by an employee must lead to dismissal.

9.   1. Breaking confidentiality: consists of releasing employee information to third parties other than the government or labor officials.
      2. Intrusive data gathering: gathering excessive personal information about an employee.
      3. Use of incorrect or outdated information on file: caused by errors that occur during input or simply outdated information.

CHAPTER 14
COMPUTERS IN THE FUTURE

SUMMARY

Robots can simply be thought of as computers with artifical limbs attached. They offer many benefits in the work place, such as working in situations too dangerous for humans or in areas where cumbersome protective devices must be used. Jobs involving nuclear-waste handling, deep sea or outer space exploration, and even repetitive precision work can use robots successfully. Sensory perception capabilities of robots will further increase the application of industrial robots. Even the ability of robots to "reproduce" themselves has been predicted by futurists.

Currently the Americans and Japanese are at the forefront of supercomputer technology. The goals are to design a computer that will perform the most computations in the fastest time and to develop artificial intelligence. The one obstacle to higher speeds is the Von Neuman bottleneck: a problem encountered when each instruction must be processed and stored sequentially at great speeds. Two methods to avoid this problem are the use of multiple machines with shared memories working in parallel, and the execution of instructions in nonsequential arrangements.

Another advancement toward increased speeds is the biochip, still highly theoretical, which uses molecules to effect a computer circuit. These tiny chips could become the brain of robots thus reducing the robot's size tremendously, or they could be implanted in humans to overcome certain physical defects.

Other more common advancements include the use of computers to monitor and enhance automobiles. The future personal computer could have a "smart" keyboard, be smaller yet more powerful, and even receive software at home via an FM radio receiver.

Software technology will also improve along with the hardware. Voice-command technology will permit a user to input commands to the computer with his or her voice. A brain-wave interface goes even further and lets a person input data via brain-waves transmitted through electrodes that are connected to the body. This capability may prove to be a major benefit to the handicapped.

Artificial intelligence will enable computers to think and reason as humans do. One approach to AI is to build expert systems where the computer is programmed to follow the same path of thinking as top experts in a particular field. In an attempt to add common sense and broaden the applications beyond that of expert systems, AI researchers are working with nonmonotonic logic theory and script theory. Nonmonotonic logic allows conclusions to be drawn from assumptions; that is, if A occurs then B will result. In contrast, script theory suggests in a particular situation that humans have a general idea of how the thinking and dialogue would proceed. This theory tries to give the computer a way to make inferences based upon the situations at hand.

To aid in the research and development of future applications of the computer, organizations such as Computer Aided Manufacturing International (CAM-I) are being developed. This is a joint effort of hardware and software companies along with aircraft, auto, and heavy-equipment manufacturers, to extend the boundaries of the growing field of CAD/CAM.

ABOUT THE ISSUE--A major concern with robots and artificial intelligence is the ethical issue involved in creating a machine with human qualities and capabilities. Will this machine be considered a form of life or just an advanced machine?

STRUCTURED LEARNING

1.   In what situations might it be advantageous for robots to work?

      a. in deep sea work
      b. in outer space
      c. with nuclear material
      d. in traditionally hazardous jobs such as underground mining
      e. all the above
      f. none of the above

      *   *   *   *   *   *   *   *   *   *   *   *

      (e) The robot can be advantageously employed in any of these work environments.

2.   What type of sensory recognition for robots is currently being explored?

      a. ESP   c. vision
      b. smell   d. telepathy

      *   *   *   *   *   *   *   *   *   *   *   *

(c) Experiments with vision are currently being conducted that convert a video image into numerical values that the computer can understand and "envision."

3.   Supercomputers currently exist with which of the following?

a.   circuitry submerged in water to permit a more rapid flow of electricity
b.   circuitry so fast and dense that refrigeration units pump coolants through them to prevent melting
c.   no possibility for further improvement
d.   all of the above
e.   none of the above

*   *   *   *   *   *   *   *   *   *   *   *

(b)   The supercomputers that currently exist must have freon-gas coolant pumped through them to avoid melting down. They still are not fast enough for some problems scientists would like to solve.

4.   Which of the following are alternatives being tried to overcome the von Neumann bottleneck in supercomputers?

a.   multiple machines with shared memory working in parallel
b.   larger supercomputers with denser curcuitry
c.   biochips replacing the microchips
d.   having the work instructions performed in non-sequential arrangements

*   *   *   *   *   *   *   *   *   *   *   *

(a) and (d) Both a and d are "non-von Neumann architectures" being experimented with in today's supercomputers.

5.   There is now a process to combine the personal computer with an FM
       broadcasting signal. What application does this offer personal
       computer users?

       a. The computer will be able to edit out all commercials and
           non-music interruptions.
       b. The computer can amplify the music in a more clear and distinct
           sound.
       c. The computer can store the songs in a digital form to play back
           later.
       d. Computer programs may be sent via FM broadcast signals to users
           at home.
       e. all of the above

       *   *   *   *   *   *   *   *   *   *   *   *

           (d) By using a specially designed FM radio receiver and audio
           cassette recorder computer programs can be recorded to use with
           the computer.

6.   What are the problems involved in creating a computer that will
       respond to the user's voice?

       a. The computer would have to store an enormous vocabulary to
           recognize everyday human conversation.
       b. Computers cannot distinguish when a word starts or stops.
       c. Computers have difficulty screening out background sounds from
           the voice commands.
       d. a and c
       e. all the above

       *   *   *   *   *   *   *   *   *   *   *   *

           (e) All of the above are problems that must be overcome before
           voice recognition becomes completely successful.

7.   Drawing conclusions from assumptions while allowing for unusual
       situations is called _____.

       a. nonmonotonic logic   c. script theory
       b. memory logic   d. expert system

       *   *   *   *   *   *   *   *   *   *   *   *

           (a) Nonmonotonic logic theory is one approach to artificial
           intelligence that is being explored.

8.   The nonprofit research and development organization, Computer Aided
     Manufacturing International (CAM-I) allows companies to participate
     in which two ways.

     a.   a set percentage of the firm's research and development funds
     b.   a substantial membership fee
     c.   through invitation only
     d.   funding of special research projects

     *   *   *   *   *   *   *   *   *   *   *   *

     (b and d) The membership fee is mandatory while the special
     funding is not. Companies can also allow their own employees
     to work on the projects to aid in the research and provide
     additional knowledge to the venture.

True/False

1.   T F   As computer and robotic capabilities increase within the work
            environment, the number of jobs that are now done by human
            beings may be reduced and some jobs eliminated entirely.

2.   T F   Robots are simply computers with limbs attached that can
            perform some of the functions of human limbs without the
            normal restrictions and limitations of humans.

3.   T F   The United States and Germany are committing large amounts of
            resources toward the development of supercomputers.

4.   T F   Some scientists are predicting that one day robots and humans
            will need to deal with potentially conflicting goals.

5.   T F   Another scientific prediction is that very tiny computers will
            be implanted in humans to correct certain body chemistry
            imbalances or physical defects.

6.   T F   No matter how far computer technology advances it will still
            be a requirement for the user to know how to program.

7.   T F   The technology of the brain-wave interface may someday help
            the deaf communicate.

8.   T F   CAM-I is a government agency involved in research and
            development.

9.   T F   Artifical intelligence is still only in the theory stage and
                actual effort towards the development of AI won't begin until
                the 1990s.

10.   T F   Reflective thought has historically set human beings apart
                from all other creatures of the world, but robots may someday
                be capable of reflective thought also.

MATCHING

a.	biochips	f.	"smart" keyboard
b.	"smart chip"	g.	expert system
c.	nonmonotonic logic	h.	script theory
d.	von Neumann bottleneck	i.	brain-wave interface
e.	CAM-I	j.	artificial intelligence

1.   One of the main problems of slowing down computer processing time is
       the _____.

2.   Scientists are attempting to grow computer chips called _____, that
       are an arrangement of molecules used to effect circuits.

3.   The _____ operates in a manner similar to a cordless telephone and
       can communicate with the main console from a distance of up to 50
       feet.

4.   Specifically built FM receivers will contain a(n) _____ to adjust
       for interference in broadcasted computer programs sent via radio
       waves.

5.   Using a(n) _____, a user can input data to a computer with brain
       waves sent via electrodes.

6.   A major effort in software development is with the creation of
       _____ which will give computers the ability to think and reason as
       humans do.

7.   A(n) _____ is designed to program the computer to follow the same
       path of thinking as top experts in a particular field.

8.   One method of creating artificial intelligence involves _____ which
       forces the computer to draw conclusions based upon a series of
       assumptions while allowing for unusual situations.

9.   The _____ is the notion that in any particular situation humans
       have an idea of how the thinking or dialogue will proceed.

10.   _____ is a nonprofit research and development organization funded by hardware and software companies along with some industrial companies.

SHORT ANSWER

1.   What are the benefits of using robots in manufacturing?

2.   What are the two areas of supercomputer research being emphasized?

3.   Explain why a biochip may offer faster processing.

4.   List some of the applications or uses the computer will offer automobiles of the future.

5.   Briefly explain the concept of script theory in regards to the field
      of artificial intelligence.

ANSWER KEY

True/False

1. T   2. T   3. F   4. T   5. T   6. F   7. T   8. F
9. F   10. T

Matching

1. d   2. a   3. f   4. b   5. i   6. j   7. g   8. c
9. h   10. e

Short Answers

1.   Robots offer many advantages such as working around the clock,
      repeating the same function with precision, and working in places
      where humans cannot work.

2.   1. attaining higher speeds
      2. developing artificial intelligence

3.   A biochip would be made up of billions of molecules and be infinitely
      smaller than a tiny silicon chip. Because the circuits would be
      shorter and packed more densely, the electric current will travel
      faster.

4.   • terminal screens mounted in the dashboard to replace dials and
        gauges
      • calculation of miles-per-gallon at any particular moment
      • estimation of arrival times
      • signalling tuneup time
      • offering computerized road maps
      • displaying a range of information detected by electronic
        sensors--cylinder compression to tire pressure to how far ahead the
        road is clear

5.   Script theory suggests that for every situation a human has a basic idea within the brain of how the thinking, dialogue or event should proceed. In other words, the computer should make inferences based on the situation at hand.

BASIC SUPPLEMENT

Section I

Introduction to BASIC

SUMMARY

The BASIC programming language was developed in the mid-1960s at
Dartmouth College by Professors John C. Kemeny and Thomas E. Kurtz. BASIC
is an acronym for Beginner's All-Purpose Symbolic Instruction Code. This
language is ideal for beginners because it is easy to learn, can be used for
a wide variety of tasks, and offers interactive capabilities. Like any
language it has rules for spelling, syntax, grammar, and punctuation. The
set of standard rules called ANSI BASIC (established by the American
National Standards Institute) has been adapted, but each manufacturer has
added special "quirks" to make use of special features of their computers.

To aid the programmer in writing the step-by-step instructions
necessary to solve a problem, there is a five-step programming process:
(1) define and document the problem, (2) design and document a solution,
(3) write and document the program, (4) submit the program to the computer,
(5) test and debug the program, and revise the documentation if necessary.
Documenting your work as you proceed will facilitate the programming process
and make later modification and updating much easier.

In defining the problem, it is easier to analyze the basic flow of
data processing--input, processing, and output--in reverse. After
determining what output is desired, a program can then be written that
"processes" the available input into the desired output.

Designing a solution requires developing a logical sequence of
instructions or statements to solve the problem analyzed in step one. A
flowchart is an effective tool for completing this step. The flowchart
symbols should be in logical order, from top down, and connected by arrows.

If the solution has been designed carefully the third step, coding the
program, follows easily. Each line of code is numbered in the sequence it is
to be executed.

The fourth step is typing the program into the computer. The computer translates the source program using either a compiler or interpreter into machine language that it can understand. A compiler will translate the entire program at once and store it in main memory for execution. The interpreter translates one line of code and then executes that line before translating the next line. This process, therefore, causes the interpreter to be the slower of the two translators. The BASIC interpreters and compilers also check for syntax errors.

The fifth step is testing the program with sample data to verify its accuracy in solving the problem. Also, the documentation is revised if necessary.

The three types of BASIC commands are: (1) program language statements, (2) system commands, and (3) editing commands. Program language statements solve the specific problems. System commands are used to communicate with the operating system of the computer. Commonly used system commands include NEW, LIST, RUN, and SAVE. System commands also control the scrolling of the program on the screen. Editing commands are used to correct mistakes or make changes within the program and are either of a screen editor or line editor type of correction.

STRUCTURED LEARNING

1.   Which of the following is not a true statement about the BASIC
      programming language?
      a. BASIC was developed in the mid-1960s.
      b. BASIC is an acronym for Basic All-Purpose Symbolic Instruction
          Code.
      c. Professors John G. Kemeny and Thomas E. Kurtz are the developers
          of the language.
      d. BASIC allows interactive communication with the computer.

      *   *   *   *   *   *   *   *   *   *   *   *

          (b) BASIC is an acronym for Beginner's All-Purpose Symbolic
          Instruction Code

2.   What is the name of the set of universally-accepted standard rules
      for the BASIC language?
      a. Applesoft BASIC   c. ANSI BASIC
      b. EBCDIC   d. The BASIC Rules

      *   *   *   *   *   *   *   *   *   *   *   *

          (c) ANSI BASIC is the standard set of rules for the BASIC language.
          It was established by the American National Standards Institute.

3.   What translator translates the entire program into machine language
      and then stores it in main memory?
      a.   interpreter   c.   compiler
      b.   syntax   d.   a and c

      *   *   *   *   *   *   *   *   *   *   *   *

         (c) The compiler translates the entire program and then stores it
         in the computer's main memory.

4.   Which of the following is not a system command?
      a.   NEW   d.   READ
      b.   SAVE   e.   RUN
      c.   LIST

      *   *   *   *   *   *   *   *   *   *   *   *

         (d) READ is a language command that is executed as the program
         runs. System commands are entered via the keyboard and executed
         immediately when the RETURN or ENTER key is depressed.

WORKSHEET

1.   What are the five steps of the programming process?

2.   Draw the symbols for a processing step, an input/output operation, and
        a terminal start/stop.

3.   True or False: GOTO, LET, and READ, are language commands the program
        uses to solve specific problems.

ANSWER KEY

Worksheet

1.   1. Define and document the problem.
        2. Design and document a solution.
        3. Write and document the program.
        4. Submit the program to the computer.
        5. Test and debug the program and revise documentation if necessary.

2.   Processing symbol

        Input/output symbol

        Terminal start/stop symbol

3.   True

Section II

Getting Started with BASIC

SUMMARY

 BASIC statements are composed of programming commands, constants,
numeric or string variables, and formulas. A BASIC program is a sequence of
these statements that tells the computer how to solve a problem. Line
numbers are used to sequence the program statements in the order in which
they are executed--from low to high. The line numbers are also used to
reference individual statements.
 Constants are values that do not change during a program's execution.
A numeric constant can either be represented as a real number or in
exponential form. Real numbers can be integers or decimal fractions but can
have no commas embedded. If the number is negative it must be preceded by a
minus sign. It will be assumed positive if there is no sign included
(e.g., 90215, -14.32, 38). Exponential form is used for very large or very
small numbers (e.g., 6.4432E+07, 1.0001E-06). Character string constants
are composed of alphanumeric data enclosed within quotation marks (e.g.,
"Ed", "8619 Willow Road").
 Variable names are assigned by the programmer and refer to data stored
in the computer's memory. The values of variable names may change as the
program is executed. The variable names may either be numeric or string.
 Numeric variable names represent a number that is either supplied by
the programmer or internally calculated by the computer during program
execution. A numeric variable must begin with a letter and be either one
letter alone or one letter followed by an alphanumeric character (e.g., A,
H2, MM).
 A string variable name represents the value of a character string.
String variable names are composed of one letter followed by a dollar sign
(e.g., N$).

The REM, LET, PRINT, and END statements are all program language statements. The REM statement provides information to anyone reading the program listing but provides no information to the computer. (General format: line # REM comment).

The LET statement is used to assign values to numeric or string variables directly or to assign the result of a calculation to a numeric variable. The value or calculated result of an expression on the right side of the equal sign is assigned to the variable on the left. (General format: line # LET variable = expression).

In BASIC, arithmetic expressions are composed of constants, numeric variables, and arithmetic operators. An arithmetic expression is performed by a hierarchy of operations: (1) operations in parentheses, (2) exponentiation, (3) multiplication or division, (4) addition or subtraction. If more than one operation is to be performed at the same level, the computer evaluates it from left to right.

The PRINT statement is used to print or display the results of computer processing. (General format: line # PRINT variables, literals, arithmetic expressions, or combination). The PRINT command will also print blank lines (e.g., line # PRINT).

The END statement indicates the end of the program and is usually assigned all 9s as the line #. This practice assures the correct location for the END command.

STRUCTURED LEARNING

1.   Which of the following sequences of line numbers would not execute the program in the order intended? (Assume the first number in the sequence is assigned to the first line of the program, etc.)
      a. 1, 2, 3, 4, 5, 6   d. 10, 20, 30, 40, 50
      b. 10, 12, 24, 36, 51   e. 19, 25, 7, 11, 15
      c. 60, 50, 40, 30, 20, 10

      *   *   *   *   *   *   *   *   *   *   *   *

      (c,e) The BASIC interpreter and compiler will put the program line numbers in sequence from low to high during translation. The computer then executes the program in this sequence.

2.   Which BASIC language command provides information for anyone reading the program but provides no information for the computer to process?
      a. PRINT   c. REM
      b. LET   d. END

      *   *   *   *   *   *   *   *   *   *   *   *

(c) The REM statement is used to document the program by explaining program segments, defining variables, or noting any special instructions.

3.   Which of the following is the correct priority of mathematical operations a computer follows?
      a. exponentiation, operations in parentheses, multiplication or division, addition or subtraction
      b. addition or subtraction, multiplication or division, exponentiation, operations in parentheses
      c. operations in parentheses, exponentiation, multiplication or division, addition or subtraction
      d. multiplication or division, addition or subtraction, exponentiation, operations in parentheses

      *   *   *   *   *   *   *   *   *   *   *   *

      (c) This is the correct priority of operations. Multiple operations at the same level are then performed left to right.

4.   Which of the following are invalid LET statements?
      a. LET A = A + 3   c. LET E1 = 5 + B$
      b. LET 3 + 12 = B   d. LET T$ = "THE END"

      *   *   *   *   *   *   *   *   *   *   *   *

      (b,c) B is invalid because the variable must be to the left of the equal sign. C is invalid because a character string variable cannot be part of an arithmetic expression.

WORKSHEET

1.   What will be printed when this program segment is keyed into the computer exactly as follows?
      10 LET X = 10
      20 PRINT X
      20 PRINT X + 5

2.   Which of the following are not valid real numbers in BASIC?   Why are
     they invalid?
     a.   .14   d.   -69
     b.   5,501   e.   .425-
     c.   19141.32   f.   1962

3.   Convert the following numbers from scientific notation to decimal
     numbers.
     a.   7.324E06   c.   9.991E-04
     b.   -2.58E03   d.   3.7294E+05

4.   Which of the following are not valid examples of a character string?
     Why are they invalid?
     a.   10 LET A$ = "EDGAR HOGE"
     b.   10 LET C$ = 304½ Conneaut Avenue
     c.   10 LET $ = "Bowling Green"
     d.   10 LET BC$ = "123-45-6789"

5.   Which of the following numeric variable names are not valid?   Why are
      they invalid?
      a.   BS   d.   H$
      b.   4   e.   TAX
      c.   A9   f.   47

6.   What is the value of each of the following numeric variables?
      a.   LET X = 4 * (5 + 3) / 2 - 3
      b.   LET A1 = ((4 / 2 - 1) + 3) * 2
      c.   LET E = 12 * 3 / 4 + (7 - 3)
      d.   LET Y4 = 6 / 2 * 3 + 9 - 2

7.   Write a line of code to print each of the following expressions.
      a.   The winner is Kowaski.   c.   999
      b.   10 + 5   d.   (a blank line)

8.   Write a line of code that uses the END statement.

PROGRAMMING PROBLEM 1

Buck Myers must drive 24 miles to his office every morning five days a week. Naturally he must also drive home the same distance. He would like to determine how far he drives to and from work in a year's time. Of the 52 weeks per year he figures he misses four weeks for vacation, holidays, and sick leave.

Buck wants his report to show how many days a year he works and also the number of miles he travels to and from work.

The output should appear as follows:

BUCK MYERS

Work days XXXX
Mileage   XXXX

PROGRAMMING PROBLEM 1 (cont.)

PROGRAMMING PROBLEM 2

Johnny Appleseed has just purchased an apple orchard and a new computer. In an effort to learn programming, he has decided to calculate how many individual apples he will pick this season and how much money he will make. Johnny's orchard has 1,200 apples trees which he estimates will average 15 bushels of apples per tree. A bushel basket holds 75 apples and each apple sells for a nickel.

He wants his report to list the number of apple trees, the total number of bushel baskets of apples, the number of individual apples he expects to pick, and finally how much money he will earn.

The output should look like this:

APPLESEED APPLE ORCHARD

Apple Trees XXXX
Bushels   XXXXX
Total Apples XXXXX
    Revenue $ XXXXX

PROGRAMMING PROBLEM 2 (cont.)

ANSWER KEY

Worksheet

1.   15 (during translation to machine language, line 20 PRINT X will be
      replaced by line 20 PRINT X + 5)

2.   b--No commas can be embedded within numbers.
      e--If the number is negative the minus sign must precede the number,
      not follow it.

3.   a. 7,324,000
      b. -2,580
      c. .0009991
      d. 372,940

4.   b--The character string must be contained within quotation marks.
      c--The character string variable must have a single letter preceding the
      dollar sign.
      d--The character string variable may have only a single letter followed
      by a dollar sign.

5.   b--It must begin with an alphabetic character.
      d--The second character must be alphanumeric (this is a character string
      variable).
      e--A variable must either be one letter or one letter followed by one
      alphanumeric character.
      f--It must begin with an alphabetic character.

6.   a. X = 13
      b. A1 = 8
      c. E = 13
      d. Y4 = 16

7.   a. 10 PRINT "The winner is Kowaski."
      b. 10 PRINT "10 + 5"
      c. 10 PRINT 999
      d. 10 PRINT

8.   9999 END

Programming Problem 1

```
10 REM *** THIS PROGRAM FIGURES THE NUMBER OF ***
20 REM *** DAYS BUCK WORKS AND THE MILES HE DRIVES.
30 REM ***
40 REM *** VARIABLE LIST ***
50 REM *** W = WEEKS PER YEAR ***
60 REM *** A = NUMBER OF WEEKS NOT WORKING ***
70 REM *** M = MILES TRAVELED PER DAY ***
80 REM *** D = NUMBER OF DAYS WORKED PER YEAR ***
90 REM *** Y = TOTAL MILES TRAVELED IN YEAR ***
100 REM ***
110 LET W = 52
120 LET A = 4
130 LET M = 48
140 LET D = (W - A) * 5
150 LET Y = D * M
160 PRINT
170 PRINT
180 PRINT "BUCK MYERS"
190 PRINT
200 PRINT "WORK DAYS",D
210 PRINT "MILEAGE",Y
9999 END


RUN


BUCK MYERS

WORK DAYS      240
MILEAGE        11520
```

Flowchart:

Start → Assign Initial Values to Variables → Calculate Days Worked Per Year → Calculate Miles Traveled Per Year → Print Report → Stop

Programming Problem 2

```
                              10 REM *** THIS PROGRAM CALCULATES THE NUMBER OF ***
   ┌─────────────┐            20 REM *** BUSHELS AND TOTAL AMOUNT OF APPLES. ***
  (   Start     )            30 REM ***
   └──────┬──────┘            40 REM *** VARIABLE LIST ***
          │                   50 REM *** T = TREES ***
   ┌──────▼──────┐            60 REM *** B = BUSHEL BASKETS PER TREE ***
  ╱ Assign       ╲           70 REM *** X = NUMBER OF APPLES PER BUSHEL ***
 ╱  Initial       ╲          80 REM *** N = TOTAL NUMBER OF BUSHELS ***
 ╲  Values to     ╱          90 REM *** A = TOTAL NUMBER OF APPLES ***
  ╲ Variables    ╱          100 REM *** R = REVENUE ***
   └──────┬──────┘           110 REM ***
          │                  120 LET T = 1200
   ┌──────▼──────┐           130 LET B = 15
   │ Calculate   │           140 LET X = 75
   │   # of      │           150 LET N = T * B
   │ Bushels of  │           160 LET A = N * X
   │ Apples      │           170 LET R = A * .05
   └──────┬──────┘           180 PRINT "APPLESEED APPLE ORCHARD"
          │                  190 PRINT
   ┌──────▼──────┐           200 PRINT "APPLE TREES",T
   │ Calculate   │           210 PRINT "BUSHELS",N
   │ Total #     │           220 PRINT "TOTAL APPLES",A
   │ of Apples   │           230 PRINT "REVENUE $",R
   └──────┬──────┘           999 END
          │
   ┌──────▼──────┐
   │ Calculate   │
   │ Revenue     │
   │             │
   └──────┬──────┘
          │
         ╱▼╲
        ╱ Print╲
        ╲Report╱            RUN
         ╲──┬─╱              APPLESEED APPLE ORCHARD
          │
   ┌──────▼──────┐           APPLE TREES     1200
  (   Stop      )           BUSHELS         18000
   └─────────────┘           TOTAL APPLES    1350000
                             REVENUE $       67500
```

Section III

Input and Output

SUMMARY

The INPUT statement is used for inquiry and response applications. It allows the user to enter data at the terminal as the program is running in a question-and-answer type environment. (General format: line # INPUT variable list). The INPUT statement is placed where the data values are needed in a program. During program execution the computer will stop and wait for the user to enter data which the computer will then assign to a variable. This statement offers flexibility to a program because the variables may be changed with each program execution.

A PRINT statement may precede the INPUT statement, prompting the user to input the desired data. The INPUT statement may also contain the prompt, within quotes, eliminating the need for a preceding PRINT command. The values inserted may be either string or numeric but must correspond to an appropriate string or numeric variable name.

Another method to input values is to use the READ and DATA commands. (General format: line # READ variable list; line # DATA constant list). The READ statement tells the computer to locate the next DATA statement and assign the data values consecutively to the variables in the READ statement. If a READ statement is attempted after the data list is exhausted an "OUT OF DATA" message is printed along with the corresponding line number of the last READ statement executed.

The READ statement, like the INPUT statement, should be located wherever the logic of the program indicates the need for data. The DATA statement is nonexecutable and therefore may be placed anywhere in the program. The BASIC compiler simply lists all the data items from all the DATA statements in order of lowest to highest line number. The order of the

READ variables and DATA values is important. The programmer must be certain the arrangement of values in the DATA statements correspond to the data required in the READ statement.

The LET, INPUT, and READ and DATA statements can all be used to enter data. The LET statement is best for situations where very little data must be entered. The INPUT statement is used when a question-and-answer environment is desired or when the data values are likely to change frequently. The READ and DATA statements are best when many data values must be entered.

The PRINT statement is used to display the results of processing. The comma and semicolon are used to control the spacing of output on the individual lines. The number of characters printed on a line varies with the system used. Also, the number and length of the print zones will vary with systems.

When a PRINT statement is encountered, the first value is printed in the first print zone. If a comma exists between the first and second variable, the second value begins in the next available print zone. If more items are listed in a PRINT statement than there are print zones, the value is printed in the first zone of the next line. A print zone may be skipped by enclosing a space in quotation marks causing the zone to appear empty or by typing two consecutive commas.

A semicolon following a variable will cause the next value to be printed in the following column, not print zone. Generally, one blank space is automatically left by the computer in front of a number for a sign. With characters a space is not left by the computer so the programmer must insert a space within the quotation marks to avoid words running together.

If a comma or semicolon follows the last variable of a list, the output from the next PRINT statement will continue on that line.

STRUCTURED LEARNING

1.   Which of the following summarize the difference between the INPUT and
        LET statements?
        a.   The INPUT statement is a system command and the LET statement a
             program language command.
        b.   The INPUT statement is an input command and the LET statement an
             output command.
        c.   The INPUT statement allows the user to enter data while the
             program is running and the LET statement does not.
        d.   none of the above

        *   *   *   *   *   *   *   *   *   *   *

             (c) The LET statement assigns a value during the program's coding
             while the INPUT statement stops the program's execution to accept
             values from the user.

2.   The READ statement _____.
      a. causes the computer to stop execution and await input from the
          user
      b. contains values to be used by the DATA statement
      c. can assign only one value per line of code
      d. causes values in the data list to be assigned to variables

      *   *   *   *   *   *   *   *   *   *   *   *

          (d) When the computer encounters a READ statement, it searches
          through the program for the DATA statements. Values in the data
          list are assigned to the variables in the READ statement.

3.   If a READ statement is attempted after the data list has been
      exhausted, the computer _____.
      a. goes back to the beginning of the data list and starts reading it
          again
      b. reads the last value of the data list repeatedly
      c. prints "OUT OF DATA IN LINE # "
      d. adopts a value of 0 for the variables

      *   *   *   *   *   *   *   *   *   *   *   *

          (c) The data list must contain at least as many values as there
          are variables to be read in the program or the OUT OF DATA
          message occurs.

4.   Which of the statements is incorrect regarding the use of LET, INPUT,
      and READ and DATA statements for input?
      a. The LET statement is used when there is very little data to
          enter.
      b. The INPUT statement is used when a question-and-answer
          environment exists.
      c. The READ and DATA statements are best when many values must be
          entered.
      d. The LET, INPUT, and READ statements are virtually interchangable
          with only a few revisions.

      *   *   *   *   *   *   *   *   *   *   *   *

          (d) The LET, INPUT, and READ and DATA statements are best
          used as statements a, b, and c summarize. They are not
          interchangeable unless major revisions are done to the program.

5.   Which of the following PRINT statements will cause the values of A1,
        A2, and A3 to be printed on one line according to the pre-defined
        print zones?
        a. 10 PRINT A1; A2; A3   d. 10 PRINT A1, A2,
        b. 10 PRINT A1 A2 A3   20 PRINT A3
        c. 10 PRINT A1, A2, A3   e. both c and d

        *   *   *   *   *   *   *   *   *   *   *   *

        (e) The comma is used to separate items that are to be printed,
        spacing these items according to the pre-defined print zones.
        When a PRINT command ending with a comma is followed by another
        PRINT command, the new ouput is started in the next available
        zone.

6.   When using a PRINT statement, _____.
        a. a character string literal must be enclosed in quotes
        b. the contents of a variable are erased after being printed
        c. the semicolon is used to print results in pre-defined print zones
        d. numeric literals must be enclosed in quotes

        *   *   *   *   *   *   *   *   *   *   *   *

        (a) Character strings must be enclosed in quotes in a PRINT
        statement. Otherwise, the computer may treat them as variable
        names.

WORKSHEET

1.   Which of the following program segments will apply these values to
      their respective variables?

$$A\$ = \text{"Butch"}$$
$$H = 72$$
$$W = 215$$

      a. 10 PRINT "Enter name, weight, height"
          20 INPUT H , W , A$
      b. 10 PRINT "Enter name, height, weight"
          20 INPUT A$, H , H
      c. 10 PRINT "Enter name, height, weight"
          20 INPUT A$, H , W

2.   Write an INPUT statement to replace each of the following lines of
      code.

      a. 10 PRINT "Enter your name"
          20 INPUT N$
      b. 10 PRINT "Enter destination and the distance in miles"
          20 INPUT D$, M

3.   Given the following DATA statement, write a READ statement to assign
      the values to variables as shown.

          80 DATA "Seymour Watt", "Director", 11 48000, 3

$$N\$ = \text{Seymour Watt}$$
$$S = 48000$$
$$T\$ = \text{Director}$$
$$E = 3$$
$$H = 11$$

4.   What values will be assigned to the variables below when the
      following program has been executed?
          10 READ   N$, A$, T, P, Z
          20 LET   T = T + 100
          30 DATA   "EDGAR", "304½ Conneaut", 700, 2, 43402
          99 END

                    N$ =
                    A$ =
                    T =
                    P =
                    Z =

5.   Suppose the value 2500 must be stored in the variables P1, P2, and
      P3. Show three different ways this can be done using LET, READ, and
      INPUT statements.

6.   Write the PRINT statement that will give each of the following lines
     of ouput.

Zone 1	Zone 2	Zone 3
a. 12	24	36
b.		
c. AB		C
d. ABC	D	E
e. John David Morrow		27

7.   The statement that allows user interaction with the computer is
     _____.

     a. READ   d. END
     b. INPUT   e. RUN
     c. DATA

8.   Which of the following programs will yield the same results?

a.   10 READ A, B
     20 READ C, D
     30 LET E = A + B + C + D
     40 PRINT E
     50 DATA 5, 6, 7, 8, 9
     99 END

c.   10 READ A, B, C, D
     20 LET E = A + B + C + D
     30 PRINT E
     40 DATA 2, 3, 4, 5
     99 END

b.   10 READ A, B, C, D
     20 LET A = A + B + C + D
     30 PRINT "E"
     40 DATA 5, 6, 7, 8
     99 END

d.   10 READ A, B, C, D
     20 LET E = A + B + C + D
     30 PRINT E
     40 DATA 5, 6
     50 DATA 7, 8
     99 END

9.   What will be the output from the following program?

```
10 READ J , A, N$
20 LET C = J * A
30 PRINT J, "$";C,
40 PRINT N$
50 DATA 40, 10.00, "Andy Thorton"
```

PROGRAMMING PROBLEM 1

The Mayday Appliance Company has an ambitious export business in its
line of washers and dryers. The company wants a program that will print out
the name of the country buying its appliances, the model numbers of its
washers and dryers being bought, and the total bill.

The necessary data for this program are as follows: Washer I--$250,
Washer II--$350, Dryer I--$175, Dryer II--$300. (Use READ and DATA
statements to input the prices.)

Run the program for a sale to Grenada of 17 Washer I's, 12 Washer II's,
21 Dryer I's, and 13 Dryer II's. (Use INPUT statements to input the number
of washers and dryers.) The output should have the following form:

MAYDAY APPLIANCE COMPANY

Sale to XXXXXXXXXXX

Number of Washers:
Model I XXXX
Model II XXXX

Number of Dryers:
Model I XXXX
Model II XXXX

Total Amount of Sale = $XXXXXX

PROGRAMMING PROBLEM 1 (cont.)

PROGRAMMING PROBLEM 2

Big Bill's Frontier Shop, in an effort to stimulate sales, has offered some outstanding specials on its products. Big Bill wants to calculate the daily sales of his most popular products--the Davey Crocket muzzleloader, Daniel Boone whistle, the Bowie knife, and Custer's last-stand hat rack. He has visions of a computer program showing daily unit sales and calculating each unit's dollar sales amount and the daily sales total for these four items.

The necessary data are the per unit sales prices: Davey Crocket muzzleloader--$75, Daniel Boone whistle--$1.50, the Bowie knife--$12, Custer's last-stand hat rack--$28. (Use READ and DATA commands to enter this information.)

Run the program using the following sales for Wednesday April 15, 198X. (Use the INPUT command to enter the amounts.)

```
Muzzleloaders   -  7 units
Whistles        - 28 units
Knives          -  3 units
Hat racks       -  0 units
```

The output should have the following form:

                    BIG BILL'S FRONTIER SHOP

TODAY'S DATE   XXXXX XX,   XXXX

TODAY'S SALES

```
ITEM                    UNITS           DOLLARS
Muzzleloaders           XXX             $ XXXXX
Whistles                XXX             $ XXXXX
Knives                  XXX             $ XXXXX
Hat racks               XXX             $ XXXXX
```

TOTAL SALES $ XXXXXX

PROGRAMMING PROBLEM 2 (cont.)

ANSWER KEY

Worksheet

1.   c

2.   a. 10 INPUT "Enter your name"; N$
      b. 10 INPUT "Enter destination, the distance in miles"; D$,M

3.   10 READ N$, T$, H, S, E

4.   N$ = EDGAR
      A$ = 304½ Conneaut
      T = 800
      P = 2
      Z = 43402

5.   10 LET P1 = 2500
      20 LET P2 = 2500
      30 LET P3 = 2500
            or
      10 READ P1, P2, P3
      20 DATA 2500, 2500, 2500
            or
      10 INPUT P1, P2, P3

6.   a. 10 PRINT 12, 24, 36
      b. 10 PRINT
      c. 10 PRINT "A"; "B", " ", "C" or 10 PRINT "A"; "B",, "C"
      d. 10 PRINT "A"; "B"; "C", "D", "E"
      e. 10 PRINT "John David Morrow", 27

7.   b

8.   a and d

9.   40 $400   ANDY THORTON

Programming Problem 1

```
Start

Enter
Prices

Enter
Country

Enter #
Units Sold
for Each
Product

Calculate
Total Sales
Revenue

Print
Sales
Report

Stop
```

```
10 REM *** THIS PROGRAM DISPLAYS THE NUMBER OF ***
20 REM *** WASHERS AND DRYERS SOLD TO A FOREIGN ***
30 REM *** COUNTRY. THE SALES TOTAL IS ALSO CALCULATED. ***
40 REM ***
50 REM *** VARIABLE LIST ***
60 REM *** C$ = NAME OF COUNTRY ***
70 REM *** W1 = WASHER I        P1 = PRICE OF WASHER I ***
80 REM *** W2 = WASHER II       P2 = PRICE OF WASHER II ***
90 REM *** D1 = DRYER I         P3 = PRICE OF DRYER I ***
100 REM *** D2 = DRYER II       P4 = PRICE OF DRYER II ***
110 REM *** T = TOTAL SALES ***
120 REM ***
130 DATA 250,350,175,300
140 READ P1,P2,P3,P4
150 REM *** ENTERING THE COUNTRY AND UNIT SALES. ***
160 INPUT "WHAT COUNTRY ARE WE SELLING TO ";C$
170 INPUT "HOW MANY MODEL I WASHERS";W1
180 INPUT "HOW MANY MODEL II WASHERS";W2
190 INPUT "HOW MANY MODEL I DRYERS";D1
200 INPUT "HOW MANY MODEL II DRYERS";D2
210 REM *** CALCULATING TOTAL SALES ***
220 LET T=P1 * W1 + P2 * W2 + P3 * D1 + P4 * D2
230 PRINT
240 PRINT
250 PRINT
260 PRINT "SALE TO ";C$
270 PRINT
280 PRINT "NUMBER OF WASHERS:"
290 PRINT "MODEL I ",W1
300 PRINT "MODEL II ",W2
310 PRINT
320 PRINT "NUMBER OF DRYERS:"
330 PRINT "MODEL I ",D1
340 PRINT "MODEL II ",D2
350 PRINT
360 PRINT "TOTAL AMOUNT OF SALE = $";T
370 END


RUN
WHAT COUNTRY ARE WE SELLING TO ? GRENADA
HOW MANY MODEL I WASHERS? 17
HOW MANY MODEL II WASHERS? 12
HOW MANY MODEL I DRYERS? 21
HOW MANY MODEL II DRYERS? 13


SALE TO GRENADA

NUMBER OF WASHERS:
MODEL I        17
MODEL II       12

NUMBER OF DRYERS:
MODEL I        21
MODEL II       13

TOTAL AMOUNT OF SALE = $ 16025
```

Programming Problem 2

```
10 REM *** THIS PROGRAM CALCULATES THE DAILY ***
20 REM *** SALES DOLLARS FOR EACH ITEM AND THE ***
30 REM *** TOTAL SALES AMOUNT ***
40 REM ***
50 REM *** VARIABLE LIST ***
60 REM *** M = MUZZLELOADER    A = PRICE OF M  ***
70 REM *** W = WHISTLE         B = PRICE OF W  ***
80 REM *** K = KNIFE           C = PRICE OF K  ***
90 REM *** H = HAT RACK        D = PRICE OF H  ***
100 REM *** M1 = DAILY SALES FOR MUZZLELOADERS ***
110 REM *** W1 = DAILY SALES FOR WHISTLES ***
120 REM *** K1 = DAILY SALES FOR KNIVES ***
130 REM *** H1 = DAILY SALES FOR HAT RACKS ***
140 REM *** D$ = TODAY'S DATE ***
150 REM *** G = TOTAL DAILY SALES AMOUNT ***
160 REM *** READING IN THE PRICES ***
170 DATA 75,1.5,12,28
180 READ A,B,C,D
190 INPUT"ENTER TODAY'S DATE";D$
200 REM *** ENTERING # SOLD AND CALCULATING SALES AMOUNT ***
210 INPUT "HOW MANY MUZZLELOADER'S SOLD";M
220 LET M1=M*A
230 INPUT "HOW MANY WHISTLE'S SOLD";W
240 LET W1=W*B
250 INPUT "HOW MANY KNIVES SOLD";K
260 LET K1=K*C
270 INPUT "HOW MANY HAT RACKS SOLD";H
280 LET H1=H*D
290 REM *** CALCULATING THE DAILY SALES TOTAL ***
300 LET G=M1+W1+K1+H1
310 REM *** PRINTING THE HEADINGS ***
320 PRINT
330 PRINT
340 PRINT "               BIG BILL'S FRONTIER SHOP"
350 PRINT
360 PRINT "TODAY'S DATE",D$
370 PRINT
380 PRINT "TODAY'S SALES"
390 PRINT
400 PRINT "ITEM","UNITS","DOLLARS"
410 PRINT "MUZZLELOADER",M,M1
420 PRINT "WHISTLE",W,W1
430 PRINT "KNIVES",K,K1
440 PRINT "HAT RACKS",H,H1
450 PRINT
460 PRINT "TOTAL SALES  $";G
470 END


RUN
ENTER TODAY'S DATE? APRIL 15 198X
HOW MANY MUZZLELOADER'S SOLD? 7
HOW MANY WHISTLE'S SOLD? 28
HOW MANY KNIVES SOLD? 3
HOW MANY HAT RACKS SOLD? 0
```

                    BIG BILL'S FRONTIER SHOP

TODAY'S DATE   APRIL 15 198X

TODAY'S SALES

ITEM	UNITS	DOLLARS
MUZZLELOADER	7	525
WHISTLE	28	42
KNIVES	3	36
HAT RACKS	0	0

TOTAL SALES $ 603

Section IV

Control Statements

SUMMARY

All BASIC programs consist of a series of statements that normally are executed in sequential order. Branching can alter the flow of execution or by-pass certain instructions. The GOTO statement is used for branching. (General format: line # GOTO transfer line #) The GOTO command is an unconditional transfer statement because the flow of execution is altered every time the statement is encountered. Instead of executing the next line after the GOTO statement the control goes to the statement indicated by the transfer line number.

Caution must be used with the GOTO statement to avoid infinite loops. If no end to the loop is specified it will keep executing indefinitely as long as there is sufficient data.

The IF/THEN statement is also used to create loops. This statement tests for a specific condition; if the condition exists, control is transferred to the line # after the THEN. (General format: line # IF expression relational symbol expression THEN line #). The conditions tested can involve either numeric or character string data. The BASIC relational symbols are < , <=> , >= , = , <>.

Trailer values and counters can both be used to control a loop execution. The trailer value is a dummy value located at the end of the data list. The IF/THEN statement is used to check for this trailer value. As long as the IF/THEN statement does not detect the trailer value the looping continues. When the trailer value is found, program control is transferred out of the loop.

The second method of controlling a loop is to create a counter which is incremented each time the loop is executed. The programmer must notify the computer of the terminal value which determines how many times the loop should be repeated. The counter is tested at the beginning of each loop to determine whether this terminal value is reached signifying that the loop has been executed the desired number of times.

STRUCTURED LEARNING

1.   Which of the following is not a true statement about the GOTO statement?
     a. It enables the program to branch.
     b. It can only be executed once per program execution.
     c. It is called an unconditional transfer statement.
     d. The flow of execution is altered every time the statement is encountered.

     *   *   *   *   *   *   *   *   *   *   *   *

          (b) The GOTO statement can be used any number of times in a computer program.

2.   In BASIC, the unconditional transfer statements include the _____.
     a. END statement   d. INPUT statement
     b. IF/THEN statement   e. b and c
     c. GOTO statement

     *   *   *   *   *   *   *   *   *   *   *   *

          (c) Unconditional transfer statements cause a branching in the flow of execution every time they are encountered. In BASIC, the GOTO statement is the only unconditional transfer statement listed.

3.   Which of the following is an invalid IF/THEN statement?
     a. 10 If J = 10 THEN 60   d. 10 IF J$ = NONE THEN 100
     b. 10 IF N = "END" THEN 60   e. b and d
     c. 10 IF X< Y THEN 40

     *   *   *   *   *   *   *   *   *   *   *   *

          (e) When making comparisons, be sure to compare like items, i.e. character strings to string variables; numerics to numeric variables.

4.   Which flowchart symbol is a decision block used to represent the IF/THEN test?

a.   c.

b.   d.

*   *   *   *   *   *   *   *   *   *   *   *

(d) The diamond-shaped symbol (◇) is the decision block, which represents the IF/THEN test.

5.   Which two of the following are techniques for loop control.
a.   trailer values   c.   counters
b.   the LET statement   d.   the GOTO statement

*   *   *   *   *   *   *   *   *   *   *   *

(a,c) A loop controlled by a trailer value contains an IF/THEN statement that checks for a value that signifies the end of data. The counter is incremented each time the loop is executed; the loop ends when the terminal value is reached.

WORKSHEET

1.   What will be the result of line 100?
      80 LET X = X + 5
      90 PRINT X
      100 GOTO 80

2.   Write a program using the GOTO statement to replace this longer
      program.
      10 DATA 5, 4, 3
      20 READ A
      30 PRINT A + 2
      40 READ A
      50 PRINT A + 2
      60 READ A
      70 PRINT A + 2
      99 END

3.   Which is the correct output for this small program?
      10 DATA 6, "CANDY", 8 "BILL", 4 "WADE"
      20 READ X, N$
      30 PRINT N$, X,
      40 GOTO 20
      99 END

      a.   6   CANDY   8   BILL   4
           WADE
           out of DATA in 20
      b.   CANDY   6
           BILL   8
           WADE   4
           out of DATA in 20
      c.   CANDY   6   BILL   8   WADE
           4
           out of DATA in 20
      d.   CANDY 6 BILL 8 WADE 4
           out of DATA in 20

4.   Given the following flowchart, write the necessary code.

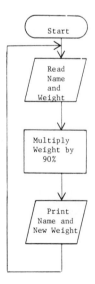

5.   What would be the result of the following two program segments?

    a.   5 DATA 3, 2, 1, 0
          10 READ X
          20 IF X< 1 THEN 99
          30 PRINT X;
          40 GOTO 10
          99 END

    b.   10 DATA "DAN", "RON", "END"
          20 READ N$
          30 IF N$ = "END" THEN 99
          40 PRINT N$
          99 END

6.   What is wrong with this program?   How can it be corrected?
      10 LET A = 2
      20 PRINT A
      30 LET A = A + 2
      40 IF A = 10 THEN 99
      50 GOTO 10
      99 END

7.   Write transfer instructions to meet the following requirement:
      a. Test to see if test score (T) is greater than 70. If so, go to
          line 220 and print name (N$) and "PASSING GRADE".
      b. Execute a loop ten times that prints your name end to end (i.e.
          OmarOmar . . . Omar)

8.   What is the final value of X?
      100 READ A
      110 LET X = 0
      120 IF A = 0 THEN 999
      130 PRINT A, X
      140 LET X = X + 1
      150 GOTO 100
      160 DATA 1, 3, 4, 0
      999 END

9.   What is wrong with the following program?
```
10 READ N$, A
20 IF N$ = "NONE" THEN 90
30 PRINT N$, A
40 LET T = T + 1
50 GOTO 10
60 DATA JOHN, 8, HOWARD, 14
70 DATA SUE, 21, ANNE, 3
80 DATA NONE
90 PRINT "TOTAL"; T
999 END
```

10.   What is the output of the following program?
```
10 LET C = 1
20 LET N$ = "Doris is a doll"
30 PRINT N$
40 LET C = C + 1
50 IF C < 6 THEN 20
99 END
```

PROGRAMMING PROBLEM 1

The basketball coach at Cloverleaf High School wants you to write a program that will display a player's name, the number of points scored, and shots missed for a game. Also it should calculate the point totals and the number of missed shots for the whole team. Last night was the first game and the results are as follows.

	Points	Missed Shots
Tony Grabowski	11	13
Scott Humble	7	7
Ron Hoge	46	3
Mark Hann	2	17
Todd Thomas	21	8
Chuck Brundage	18	0

Use the READ/DATA statement to enter the player's name, points, and misses.

The output should appear as follows:

CLOVERLEAF HIGH SCHOOL

Player	Points	Missed Shots
XXXXXXXX	XXX	XXX
XXXXXXXX	XXX	XXX
XXXXXXXX	XXX	XXX
XXXXXXXX	XXX	XXX
XXXXXXXX	XXX	XXX
XXXXXXXX	XXX	XXX

Total team points for game is XXX

Total team missed shots for game is XXX

PROGRAMMING PROBLEM 1 (cont.)

PROGRAMMING PROBLEM 2

The Imperial Society of Change Counters has dipped into its meager
treasury account and purchased a microcomputer. To compensate for this
expenditure, President Leagon has established a membership tax on the club
members' savings accounts. Any member with under $500 in savings will pay
$25, those with savings accounts greater than $500 but less than $1,500 pay
a 20 percent contribution, and those with over $1,500 will pay a 30 percent
contribution.

The member's names and savings account balances are as follows.

```
Buchanon        $  350
Lincoln         $   58
Washington      $  505
Kennedy         $1,700
Leagon          $3,000
Jefferson       $1,100
Grant           $  750
Roosevelt       $  225
Nixon           $  900
```

Each member's name, savings account balance, and contribution should
be printed. The total number of members for each of the three contribution
groups should be figured. Finally, the total contribution for all members
is required.

The output should appear as follows:

IMPERIAL SOCIETY OF CHANGE COUNTERS

Member	Savings	Contribution
XXXXXX	$XXXXX	$XXXXX
XXXXXX	$XXXXX	$XXXXX
XXXXXX	$XXXXX	$XXXXX
XXXXXX	$XXXXX	$XXXXX
XXXXXX	$XXXXX	$XXXXX
XXXXXX	$XXXXX	$XXXXX
XXXXXX	$XXXXX	$XXXXX
XXXXXX	$XXXXX	$XXXXX
XXXXXX	$XXXXX	$XXXXX

```
Total number of members  <  $500 is XXX
Total number of members  >  $500 and <  $1,500 is XXX
Total number of members  >  $1,500 is XXX

The total contribution    $XXXXXX
```

PROGRAMMING PROBLEM 2 (cont.)

ANSWER KEY

Worksheet

1.   Program execution will go to line 80.

2.    ```
10 DATA 5, 4, 3
20 READ A
30 PRINT A + 2
40 GOTO 20
99 END
```

3.    c

4.    ```
10 DATA
20 READ N$, W
30 LET P = W * .90
40 PRINT N$, P
50 GOTO 20
99 END
```

5.   a. 3 2 1
      b. DAN
          RON

6.   Line 50 unconditionally sends control to line 10. As a result, A never reaches the value of 10. This makes an infinite loop. Line 50 should be 50 GOTO 20.

7.   a.   ```
10 IF T > 70 THEN 220
      .
      .
      .
220 PRINT N$, "PASSING GRADE"
```
      b.  ```
10 LET X = 1
20 IF X > 10 THEN 99
30 PRINT "OMAR";
40 LET X = X + 1
50 GOTO 20
99 END
```

8.   X = 0

9.   Since line 10 reads two values, there should also be two trailer values included in the DATA statements. Otherwise, an error will result.

10.   DORIS IS A DOLL
        DORIS IS A DOLL
        DORIS IS A DOLL
        DORIS IS A DOLL
        DORIS IS A DOLL

Programming Problem 1

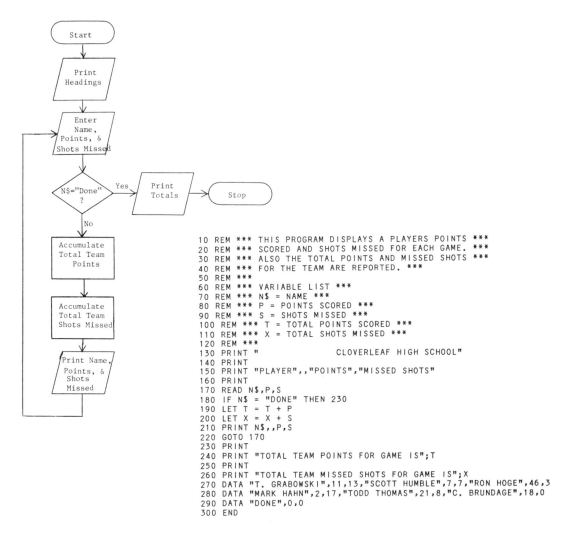

```
10 REM *** THIS PROGRAM DISPLAYS A PLAYERS POINTS ***
20 REM *** SCORED AND SHOTS MISSED FOR EACH GAME. ***
30 REM *** ALSO THE TOTAL POINTS AND MISSED SHOTS ***
40 REM *** FOR THE TEAM ARE REPORTED. ***
50 REM ***
60 REM *** VARIABLE LIST ***
70 REM *** N$ = NAME ***
80 REM *** P = POINTS SCORED ***
90 REM *** S = SHOTS MISSED ***
100 REM *** T = TOTAL POINTS SCORED ***
110 REM *** X = TOTAL SHOTS MISSED ***
120 REM ***
130 PRINT "          CLOVERLEAF HIGH SCHOOL"
140 PRINT
150 PRINT "PLAYER",,"POINTS","MISSED SHOTS"
160 PRINT
170 READ N$,P,S
180 IF N$ = "DONE" THEN 230
190 LET T = T + P
200 LET X = X + S
210 PRINT N$,,P,S
220 GOTO 170
230 PRINT
240 PRINT "TOTAL TEAM POINTS FOR GAME IS";T
250 PRINT
260 PRINT "TOTAL TEAM MISSED SHOTS FOR GAME IS";X
270 DATA "T. GRABOWSKI",11,13,"SCOTT HUMBLE",7,7,"RON HOGE",46,3
280 DATA "MARK HAHN",2,17,"TODD THOMAS",21,8,"C. BRUNDAGE",18,0
290 DATA "DONE",0,0
300 END
```

```
RUN
               CLOVERLEAF HIGH SCHOOL

PLAYER                      POINTS          MISSED SHOTS

T. GRABOWSKI                11              13
SCOTT HUMBLE                7               7
RON HOGE                    46              3
MARK HAHN                   2               17
TODD THOMAS                 21              8
C. BRUNDAGE                 18              0

TOTAL TEAM POINTS FOR GAME IS 105

TOTAL TEAM MISSED SHOTS FOR GAME IS 48
```

Programming Problem 2

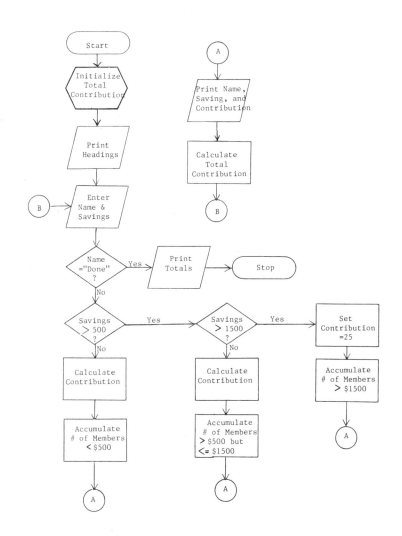

```
10 REM *** THIS PROGRAM CALCULATES THE CONTRIBUTION ***
20 REM *** CHARGE FOR EACH MEMBER BASED ON HIS SAVINGS ***
30 REM *** ACCOUNT BALANCE. THE TOTAL CONTRIBUTION IS ***
40 REM *** ALSO CALCULATED. ***
50 REM ***
60 REM *** VARIABLE LIST ***
70 REM *** N$ = NAME                                    ***
80 REM *** S = SAVINGS                                  ***
90 REM *** C = CONTRIBUTION                             ***
100 REM *** M1 = MEMBERS <= $500                        ***
110 REM *** M2 = MEMBERS > $500 BUT <= $1500            ***
120 REM *** M3 = MEMBERS > $1500                        ***
130 REM *** T = TOTAL CONTRIBUTION                      ***
140 REM ***
150 LET T = 0
154 PRINT
155 PRINT "IMPERIAL SOCIETY OF CHANGE COUNTERS"
158 PRINT
160 PRINT "MEMBER","SAVINGS","CONTRIBUTION"
170 PRINT
180 READ N$,S
190 REM *** CHECKING FOR THE END OF DATA LIST ***
200 IF N$ = "DONE" THEN 380
210 IF S > 500 THEN 260
220 LET C = 25
230 LET M1 = M1 + 1
240 GOTO 340
250 REM *** CALCULATING MEMBERS > $500 BUT <= $1500 ***
260 IF S > 1500 THEN 310
270 LET C = S * .2
280 LET M2 = M2 + 1
290 GOTO 340
300 REM *** CALCULATING MEMBERS > $1500
310 LET C = S * .3
320 LET M3 = M3 + 1
330 REM *** PRINTING INDIVIDUAL LINE AND ADDING TOTAL CONTRIBUTION ***
340 PRINT N$,"$";S,"$";C
350 LET T = T + C
360 GOTO 180
370 REM *** PRINTING TOTALS ***
380 PRINT
390 PRINT "TOTAL NUMBER OF MEMBERS <= $500 IS";M1
400 PRINT "TOTAL NUMBER OF MEMBERS > $500 BUT <= $1500 IS";M2
410 PRINT "TOTAL NUMBER OF MEMBERS > $1500 IS";M3
420 PRINT
430 PRINT "THE TOTAL CONTRIBUTION IS $";T
440 DATA "BUCHANAN",350,"LINCOLN",58,"WASHINGTON",505,"KENNEDY",1700
450 DATA "LEAGON",3000,"JEFFERSON",1100,"GRANT",750,"ROOSEVELT",225
460 DATA "NIXON",900,"DONE",0
470 END


RUN

IMPERIAL SOCIETY OF CHANGE COUNTERS

MEMBER          SAVINGS         CONTRIBUTION

BUCHANAN        $ 350           $ 25
LINCOLN         $ 58            $ 25
WASHINGTON      $ 505           $ 101
KENNEDY         $ 1700          $ 510
LEAGON          $ 3000          $ 900
JEFFERSON       $ 1100          $ 220
GRANT           $ 750           $ 150
ROOSEVELT       $ 225           $ 25
NIXON           $ 900           $ 180

TOTAL NUMBER OF MEMBERS <= $500 IS 3
TOTAL NUMBER OF MEMBERS > $500 BUT <= $1500 IS 4
TOTAL NUMBER OF MEMBERS > $1500 IS 2

THE TOTAL CONTRIBUTION IS $ 2136
```

Section V

FOR/NEXT Loops and Functions

SUMMARY

    The FOR and NEXT statements are another method of loop control. These
statements allow concise loop definition. (General format: line # FOR loop
variable = initial value TO terminal value STEP step value) (line # NEXT
loop variable.)

    The FOR statement defines how many times the loop is to be executed.
The loop variable is first set to an initial value. This value is tested
against the terminal value each time the statement is executed to determine
whether to continue the loop or direct execution to the line immediately
after the NEXT statement. The step value specifies the value to be added to
the initial value after each FOR/NEXT loop is executed. (If the step value
is omitted from the FOR statement, the value 1 will automatically be added
to the initial value.)

    The NEXT statement increments the loop variable by the amount of the
step value. It also transfers control back to the FOR statement at which
time the new value of the loop variable is compared to the terminal value.

    The following rules apply to the use of the FOR and NEXT statements.

1. A negative step value may be used. If used, the initial value
   must be greater than the terminal value.
2. The step value should never be zero.
3. Transfer can be made from one statement to another within a loop
   but never from within the loop to the FOR statement.
4. The value of the loop variable should not be modified by program
   statements within the loop.
5. The initial, terminal and step expressions can be composed of any
   valid numeric variable, constant, or mathematical formula.
6. Each FOR statement must be accompanied by an associated NEXT
   statement which contains the same loop variable.

Some ANSI standard library functions have been built into the BASIC language to alleviate the need for programmers to code these functions. (General format: function name (argument)). Programmers may simply insert these functions in place of constants, variables, or expressions in BASIC statements.

The definition statement allows the programmer to define a function not already included in the BASIC language. (General format: line # DEF function name (argument) = expression). The function name consists of FN followed by one other letter. The arithmetic expression is limited to one line of code.

STRUCTURED LEARNING

1.   When FOR/NEXT statements are used for loop control, the variable whose value is to be changed each time the loop is executed appears in _____.
    a.   the FOR statement
    b.   a REM statement preceding the loop
    c.   the NEXT statement
    d.   both the FOR and NEXT statements

    *   *   *   *   *   *   *   *   *   *   *   *

        (d) The variable is indicated in both the FOR and NEXT statements. For example: 10 FOR I = 1 to 5

                            .
                            .
                            .
                        40 NEXT I
        When the FOR statement is executed the first time, it sets the loop control variable I to 1 (the indicated initial value) and tests to see if the value of I has exceeded the indicated terminal value (5 in this case). When the NEXT statement is executed, the computer adds the step value to the value of the loop control variable and returns command to the FOR statement.

2.   The step size used in a FOR statement _____.
    a.   is always one   c.   cannot be negative
    b.   is always positive   d.   cannot be zero

    *   *   *   *   *   *   *   *   *   *   *   *

(d) The number following the word STEP tells the computer how much the value of the loop control variable is to change each time the loop is executed. If the STEP clause is omitted, the step value is assumed to be one. The step value can also be negative. However, the step size should never be zero; this would cause the computer to loop an endless number of times.

3. Which of the following does not occur when a FOR statement is executed?
    a. The loop control variable is set to the indicated initial value.
    b. The value of the variable is tested to see if it has already exceeded the indicated terminal value.
    c. The step value is added to the value of the loop control variable.
    d. The statements in the loop are executed if the value of the variable has not exceeded the terminal value.

*   *   *   *   *   *   *   *   *   *   *   *

(c) The step value is added to the value of the loop control variable when the NEXT statement is executed.

4. What will the following program print when it is run?
```
10 LET A = 2
20 FOR I = 5 to 1 STEP -2
30    PRINT I * A,
40 NEXT I
99 END
```
    a. 10 6 2   c. 5
                                            3
                                            1
    b. 10   6   2   d. 5   3   1

*   *   *   *   *   *   *   *   *   *   *   *

(b) The initial value of the loop control variable I is 5 and it is decreased by 2 each time the loop is executed until it is less than 1. Thus, I will be equal to 5, 3, and 1 during the execution of the loop. Since A is always equal to 2, PRINT I * A will cause 10, 6, and 2 to be printed. Since the PRINT statement ends with a comma, the new value will be started in the next available print zone.

5.   Given the following nested loop, how many times will the inner loop
        be executed?
             10 FOR I = 1 to 5
             20   FOR J = 6 to 15
             30   PRINT I, J
             40   NEXT J
             50 NEXT I
             99 END
        a. 15   c. 21
        b. 50   d. 30

        *   *   *   *   *   *   *   *   *   *   *   *

            (b) The outer loop will be executed 5 times since I varies from
            1 to 5. The inner loop will be executed 10 times (J varies from
            6 to 15) each time the outer loop is executed. Thus, the inner
            loop will be executed a total of 50 times.

WORKSHEET

1.   Write the FOR/NEXT statement and coding to replace the following
        short program.
             10 LET X = 3
             20 IF X > 15 THEN 99
             30 PRINT X - 1, X + 1
             40 LET X = X + 2
             50 GOTO 20
             99 END

2.   What will be the output from the following program segments?
     a. 10 FOR J = 5 to 15 STEP 5   c.   10 FOR N = 6 to 1 STEP -1
         20   PRINT J * 2,   20   PRINT N
         30 NEXT J   30 NEXT N
         40 PRINT "THAT'S ALL"   99 END
         99 END
     b. 10 FOR L = 6 to 18 STEP 3
         20   PRINT "$*";
         30 NEXT L
         99 END

3.   What is the loop variable, the initial value, the terminal value, and
     the step value in the following flowchart symbol?

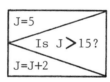

4.   Write a program derived from the following flowchart.

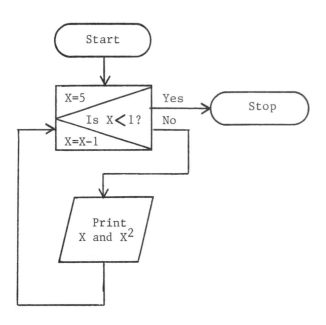

5.   Explain why the following FOR/NEXT loops are invalid and make a
     correction.
     a.   10 FOR I = 10 to 1 STEP 0   c.   10 FOR K = 1 to 10 STEP -2
          .   20   LET T = K + 4
          .   30 NEXT K
          .   d.   10 FOR N = 1 to 1000
          50 NEXT I   20   LET X = 3 * N
     b.   10 FOR J = 1 to 5   30   LET N = N / X
          20   LET K = J / 10 + 2   40   PRINT N
          30   PRINT K   50 NEXT N
          40   GOTO 10
          50 NEXT J

6.   Which of the following programs will compute the average price (A) of
       5 books?
       a.   10 FOR N = 1 to 5
            20   LET T = 0
            30   READ P
            40   LET T = T + P
            50   LET A = T / 5
            60 NEXT N
            70 PRINT A
            80 DATA 5.95, 1.98, 2.50, 3.69, 1.50
            99 END
       b.   10 LET T = 0
            20 FOR N = 1 to 5
            30   READ P
            40   LET T = T + P
            50 NEXT N
            60 LET A = T / 5
            70 PRINT A
            80 DATA 5.95, 1.98, 2.50, 3.69, 1.50
            99 END

7.   Write the line of code to define the function: $(X + 5 \wedge 2) * 3 / 4$.
       Name the function FNA.

PROGRAMMING PROBLEM 1

    Mr. and Mrs. Evans have been having a difficulty saving money. One
night Mr. Evans decided they had to start saving money slowly by saving
pennies. One Monday he put 1 cent in his bank, on Tuesday 2 cents, on
Wednesday 4 cents, on Thursday 8 cents, and Friday 16 cents. (In general,
he put in twice the previous day's savings.) So far he had saved 31 cents.
When Mrs. Evans saw the savings account balance on Friday afternoon, she
broke into a fit of laughter and ridiculed her husband for being so simple
minded. Mr. Evans was convinced that his penny-saving strategy would
produce savings, even though meager, and vowed to continue saving pennies in
this manner for 30 days. Write a program that will convince Mrs. Evans that
the pennies will add up to a substantial amount. Start calculating the
daily and total savings beginning with the sixth day since we know Mr. Evans
has already saved 31 cents.

    The following output is required for this problem:

DAY	SAVINGS	TOTAL SAVINGS
6	$XXXXX	$XXXXXXXX
7	$XXXXX	$XXXXXXXX
.	$XXXXX	$XXXXXXXX
.	$XXXXX	$XXXXXXXX
.	$XXXXX	$XXXXXXXX
30	$XXXXX	$XXXXXXXX

PROGRAMMING PROBLEM 1 (cont.)

PROGRAMMING PROBLEM 2

    Andy is just learning his multiplication tables. His father has just
bought him a microcomputer and wants you to write a program to help teach
Andy these tables. The program should permit Andy to input any number into
the program. The computer will print out the equations and answers to that
number when multiplied by the numbers 1 through 9. The program should
continue prompting Andy to enter new numbers until he decides to end the
program.

    The following output is required for this problem:

Multiplication Table for Number X
XX * 1 = XXX
XX * 2 = XXX
      .
      .
      .
XX * 9 = XXX

PROGRAMMING PROBLEM 2 (cont.)

ANSWER KEY

Worksheet

1.   10 FOR X = 3 to 15 STEP 2
      20   PRINT X - 1, X + 1
      30 NEXT X
      99 END

2.   a. 10   20   30   THAT'S ALL
      b. $*$*$*$*$*$*
      c. 6
         5
         4
         3
         2
         1

3.   Loop variable = J
      Initial value = 5
      Terminal value = 15
      Step value = 2

4.   10 FOR X = 5 to 1 STEP -1
      20   PRINT X, X^2
      30 NEXT X
      99 END

5.   a. When the step size is zero, the computer will loop an endless
         number of times. This error condition is known as an infinite
         loop.

      Correction: 10 FOR I = 10 to 1 STEP -1 (Any negative number is
                   correct.)

      b. Transfer from a statement within a loop to the FOR statement of
         the loop is illegal. The transfer would cause the loop control
         variable J to be reset to 1 and form an infinite loop.

      Correction: Eliminate line 40 or have the GOTO statement transfer
                   control to the NEXT statement.

      c. When the step size is negative, the initial value of the loop
         control variable must be greater than the terminal value.

      Correction: either 10 FOR K = 1 to 10 STEP 2
                      or 10 FOR K = 10 to 1 STEP -2

      d. The value of the loop variable should not be modified by program statements within the loop.

Correction: 20 LET X = 3 * N
                30 LET D = N / X
                40 PRINT D

6.   b

7.   10 DEF FNA(X) = (X + 5 ∧ 2) * 3 / 4

Programming Problem 1

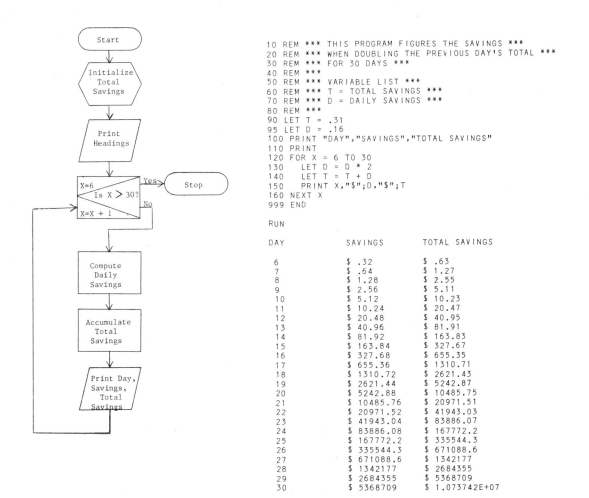

```
10 REM *** THIS PROGRAM FIGURES THE SAVINGS ***
20 REM *** WHEN DOUBLING THE PREVIOUS DAY'S TOTAL ***
30 REM *** FOR 30 DAYS ***
40 REM ***
50 REM *** VARIABLE LIST ***
60 REM *** T = TOTAL SAVINGS ***
70 REM *** D = DAILY SAVINGS ***
80 REM ***
90 LET T = .31
95 LET D = .16
100 PRINT "DAY","SAVINGS","TOTAL SAVINGS"
110 PRINT
120 FOR X = 6 TO 30
130    LET D = D * 2
140    LET T = T + D
150    PRINT X,"$";D,"$";T
160 NEXT X
999 END

RUN

DAY             SAVINGS          TOTAL SAVINGS

6               $ .32            $ .63
7               $ .64            $ 1.27
8               $ 1.28           $ 2.55
9               $ 2.56           $ 5.11
10              $ 5.12           $ 10.23
11              $ 10.24          $ 20.47
12              $ 20.48          $ 40.95
13              $ 40.96          $ 81.91
14              $ 81.92          $ 163.83
15              $ 163.84         $ 327.67
16              $ 327.68         $ 655.35
17              $ 655.36         $ 1310.71
18              $ 1310.72        $ 2621.43
19              $ 2621.44        $ 5242.87
20              $ 5242.88        $ 10485.75
21              $ 10485.76       $ 20971.51
22              $ 20971.52       $ 41943.03
23              $ 41943.04       $ 83886.07
24              $ 83886.08       $ 167772.2
25              $ 167772.2       $ 335544.3
26              $ 335544.3       $ 671088.6
27              $ 671088.6       $ 1342177
28              $ 1342177        $ 2684355
29              $ 2684355        $ 5368709
30              $ 5368709        $ 1.073742E+07
```

Programming Problem 2

```
10 REM *** THIS PROGRAM HELPS ANDY ***
20 REM *** LEARN HIS MULTIPLICATION TABLES ***
30 REM ***
40 REM *** VARIABLE LIST ***
50 REM *** D$ = INPUT VARIABLE TO CONTINUE ***
60 REM *** N = NUMBER ENTERED ***
70 INPUT "ENTER A NUMBER ANDY" ; N
80 PRINT
90 PRINT
100 PRINT
110 PRINT "MULTIPLICATION TABLE FOR NUMBER " ; N
120 PRINT
130 FOR I = 1 TO 9
140    PRINT N ;"x" ; I ; " =" ; N * I
150 NEXT I
160 PRINT
170 PRINT
180 PRINT "TYPE Y IF YOU WANT TO CONTINUE"
190 PRINT "TYPE N IF YOU WANT TO STOP"
200 INPUT D$
210 IF D$ = "N" THEN 230
220 GOTO 70
230 END


RUN
ENTER A NUMBER ANDY? 5


MULTIPLICATION TABLE FOR NUMBER   5

    5  x  1   = 5
    5  x  2   = 10
    5  x  3   = 15
    5  x  4   = 20
    5  x  5   = 25
    5  x  6   = 30
    5  x  7   = 35
    5  x  8   = 40
    5  x  9   = 45


TYPE Y IF YOU WANT TO CONTINUE
TYPE N IF YOU WANT TO STOP
? N
```

†